C01

An Enigma of Ancient Suffolk

South Elmham Before 1066

An Enigma of Ancient Suffolk

South Elmham Before 1066

By

Basil Harrold

2003

First Published in 2003 by Red Bird Press
Kiln Farm, Brightlingsea, Colchester, Essex CO7 0SX

Copyright © 2003 Basil Harrold
ISBN No. 1-902626-57-5

Contents

List of Plates

List of Figures

List of Maps

List of Tables

Plate I

Elm Cottage All Saints

Photographed by the author in the Spring of 1953

Introduction

South Elmham lies fifteen miles inland on the northern boundary of Suffolk. It has a unity given to it by the saintly names of its parishes, and its compact rectangular shape. It retains much of its ancient form, and has the deep mysteries of the Saxon bishopric, and its ruined Old Minster lying within a large earthen rampart. Like most of Suffolk, it has old hedgerows brilliantly decorated with flowers in spring, and heavy with autumnal fruit. These hedges conceal medieval farmhouses, some with modern facades, but still supported by their ancient timber frames.

It has an area of about 14 square miles, forming a quarter (or ferding) of the old hundred of Wangford, and its nine parishes were, for eight hundred years, a separate deanery. South Elmham lies mostly on the boulder clay plateau of northern Suffolk. The river Waveney forms its northwest boundary as it meanders down a broad valley. A small tributary joins this river near its southwest corner, and forms a wide arc through the landscape. This tributary, called The Beck, rises in the high ground of the parish of St. James and runs first northeast, then, for part of its course, forms the boundary between South Elmham and Rumburgh. As it turns north and then to the west it forms a deep valley in the villages of St. Peter and St. Cross. The high land in St James, at about 175 feet above sea level, forms the watershed between the rivers Waveney and Blyth. (See Map III) Here the freshly ploughed clay lies in great slabs awaiting the harrow, and after the harrow the tilth lies flat and spotted by innumerable flints. Heavy rain moves reluctantly into the soil, or runs off into the system of ditches, which for most of the year are dry. In the second half of the 20th century field sizes have increased at the expense of hedges and ditches, farms have increased in acreage releasing many farmhouses with their yards, to non-farming use. Some of the most isolated old houses have gone within living memory, such as Elm Cottage in All Saints (see Plate 1), and Donna Farm on Uncle's Lane in St Michael. Dutch elm disease has deprived the scene of many of its greatest trees, the giant boles of some of these still lie above the site of Elm Cottage.

Charles Bird (1862 –1950), whom I had known in the 1930's and 40's, had lived in Elm Cottage, many years earlier. He was able to recall memories of the Reverend Samuel Blois Turner, Rector of All Saints for 20 years from 1862. Snippets of P.H.Harrold's* shorthand record of some of these memories as recounted by Charles are a good illustration of the profound social and physical changes that can occur over a period of 130 years. "*Mr. Turner was a nice man, he was short and thick and had a short neck. He died on the first of November suddenly, they was cutting bushes for the gunpowder plot. Mrs Turner was tall and slender like. She was more stern like, and you mustn't pass them without a bow or a curtsey. The women used to nearly sit down on the road, they used to bob down, they did.*" Then he said of Mr. Smith-Rewse, rector of St. Margaret for 30 years from 1886, "*if they didn't bow he used to tell them of it. He was a very stern man, he was: austere he was. Anyone courting in Saint Magaret's they darsen't for their life go arm in arm, he'd tell em of it in a minute. They had to walk one on one side of the road, and one on the other. Yes, but after his wife died he married again in six months so I've heard say.*" Talking of Mr. Newsome and his ownership of Mill Farm on All Saints Common, he said: "*there used to be a tower mill there. In 1879, that wet summer, there was wind and wet and my father looked out of the window and he say 'why the old mill's blown down'. The whole top come off, and the whole four sails come on to the ground. There was a horse in the mill yard and that didn't hurt that.*" Remembering another relic of All Saints common he said; "*there used to be a gate across the road just outside the drive;* (to the Old Rectory) *there was another gate down by Rumburgh Vicarage*". These physical and social changes, within two lifetimes, are indications of the difficulties of attempting an interpretation of the ancient history of the district. Nevertheless, an attempt will be made in the following pages to highlight the most enduring features of the landscape, and describe what is known of its ancient human history up to the time of the Norman Conquest.

My inspiration for this account of South Elmham has come from a long acquaintance with the place, and from reading the historical works of Alfred Suckling, John Raven, Rainbird Clarke, Norman Scarfe, Peter Warner, and others. These influences have tempted me to pursue an interest particularly into the Saxon heyday of the district and its bishopric. The early see of Elmham has almost no written history and scanty archaeological markers, so what chance has the reader of finding any answers in this text?

What follows is a collection of some of the primary source, and archaeological evidence, with various interpretations and no doubt distortions, including my own. The collection of some of this information

*P.H.Harrold, owned The Old Rectory All Saints From 1936-1972.

has involved enjoyable visits, to many English villages, and to Scandinavian and other European sites. The account is inevitably disjointed, and at times discursive. My conclusions come to the reader without the influence of any expert historical adviser. I emphasise this because my own training has been in science and medicine. Avoiding expert criticism before publication may have been foolhardy, but it will allow the reader to have an independent, even if inexpert, view of the ancient history, and long forgotten importance of this part of Suffolk.

Most of the illustrations, photographs, and tables, are my own. The origin of those that are not, are stated beside them. I am indebted to my wife for her constant encouragement, and to her and the family for their patience, and for their help in reading and correcting the proofs. William Harrold gave me essential assistance in calculating the orientation of an ancient sunrise at The Old Minster.

Basil Harrold. M.D. F.R.C.P.
Halesworth, 2003

An Enigma of Ancient Suffolk

Chapter I

From the last Ice Age to the earliest evidence of human activity

A few words on the formation of the local landscape.

The thick layer of boulder clay that covers most of the area is a moraine. This was deposited by glaciation during the last Ice Age, on bedrock of crag. Crag is sandy marine sediment, often full of well-preserved fossil shells, which can be seen well in the cliffs at Walton on The Naze, and at Bawdsey, but it lies many feet beneath the clay in South Elmham. Beneath the crag is a layer of chalk, and its upward tilt to the west makes it visible in the cliffs of northwest Norfolk.

The boulder clay above the crag has two origins. One is the Corton formation of sands, gravels and clays, named after its coastal outcrop at Corton just north of Lowestoft. These deposits were carried here on the Scandinavian ice sheet, which entered the area from just east of north. Above this and forming much of the surface layers in our district is the Lowestoft till formation, again of sands, gravels and clay. These deposits came from the central uplands of Britain. As the ice melted, the river Waveney resumed its preglacial valley. Its source was not in the Fens, but in the hills of the west midlands and the southern Pennines; this "proto Waveney" has been called the Bytham River. Its outwash formed an extensive gravel terrace in Flixton where The Hall once stood, and where the gravel is now being quarried.

During the Recent, or Holocene Epoch, (from about 11,000 years ago) faltering, yet progressive improvement in the climate led to melting of the ice sheets covering much of northern Europe, and a consequent rise in sea level. This was gradual, and considerable. Between 8,700 and 4,500 years ago the rise was between 22 and 26 metres. This had a profound influence on the river valleys, which were much deeper than they are now, and would have had steeper sides. The rising sea level would have slowed the flow and made the lower reaches brackish. In the Waveney valley evidence of ancient salt marshes have been found as far upstream as Beccles. This slowing of the river flow caused silting, and the development of the broad flat-bottomed fertile valley that now forms the northwest boundary of South Elmham. Whatever the waterway itself was used for, one of its most important functions for early man would have been to act as a route marker to other settlements, and to the sea.

Some scanty evidence for the nature of the local prehistoric flora and fauna.

Information on the prehistoric vegetation and animal life of the Waveney valley and its surroundings is sparse indeed. One undated sample, among many taken from the Flixton quarry, did contain pollen. Examination of this sample, taken in 1954, revealed the following pollens: sedges 24%, grasses 22%, pinks 17%, birch 11%, pine 10%, willow 3%, spruce 3%, others 10%. [2] Mammalian remains were found in the upper Flixton gravel by Funnell in 1955 [3]. These included mammoth, woolly rhinoceros, giant elk, horse, bison, and reindeer. These botanical and mammalian finds were considered to be from a post Anglian interglacial cold period. [4]

Twelve miles upstream from Flixton a further opportunity for archaeological investigation came when the Scole/Stuston bypass was under construction at Oakley. Here examination of the silt in an ancient channel of the Waveney was most rewarding, giving the best dated pollen sequence from Bronze Age to Saxon periods in the region. [5] In deposits dated 1530-1300 BC (Bronze Age) the site was heavily wooded. Tree and shrub pollens formed 88% of the total; these were dominated by lime, oak, and hazel, with scattered elms. The presence of ivy, holly, and willow, suggests some patchy opening of the canopy. On the other hand, high values for fern spores show that there were also densely shaded areas. In the next more recent layer of silt there was a sudden change in the pollen types, suggesting that there had been some loss or truncation of the sequence, perhaps by erosion. This layer had radio carbon dating coming forward to 370 BC, (Iron Age) and showed a decline in tree and shrub pollens to only 35% of the total. Lime pollen had almost gone, and oak and hazel was greatly reduced. Even alder had declined. Beech, which was not found in the earlier silt, appeared as a small proportion of the total, and birch and ash increased slightly. By far the most obvious change was an increase in grasses, which now made up between 20 and 35% of the total, and the presence of ribwort plantain, and other grassland herbs that indicate pastureland. It was also at this time that cereal pollens began to appear, and with them poppies and cornflowers. Interpretation of radio carbon dating is full of pitfalls, but the authors conclude that this part of the Waveney valley was probably quite open in the early part of the Iron Age, and that this openness, though a little variable, persisted. Without any more local information it is likely, that similar changes were taking place in the South Elmham stretch of the Waveney valley. How far this would have extended into the higher and heavier land is not known.

Evidence of pre-Roman human settlement.

Aerial photography has proved to be an irreplaceable method of initial recognition of ancient human activity. By demonstrating changes in the vigour of growing crops and differences in soil colour not appreciated at ground level, the method may reveal earthworks from the Stone Age to the 20th century. So it was for South Elmham, when in 1976 four ring ditches were discovered by aerial photography on the Flixton gravel terrace[6]. (See Map V) These ring ditches were later shown to be the ploughed out remains of Bronze Age round barrows. Publication of the results of an excavation of one of these appeared twenty-one years later in a painstakingly detailed report[7]. The excavation had been prompted by the use of the site for gravel extraction, and therefore its impending destruction.

The gravel terrace, on which archaeological finds were made, was that part of Flixton formed by the glacial outwash of the ancient Bytham River. It forms a high, firm, dry site overlooking the River Waveney. The interest in the Bronze Age ring ditch led to the quite unexpected discovery of Neolithic postholes. These postholes antedated the ring ditch by about 750 years, and are so far unique in Suffolk.

After more stripping of the topsoil, these Neolithic postholes and some pits were shown to form a roughly circular enclosure about 18 metres in diameter with a 3 metres opening to the northwest. (See Figure 1) A rectangular posthole arrangement in the centre was aligned with the opening. The 36 postholes now looked like a poorly laid out circle, but with a northwest-southeast line of symmetry. It has been suggested that the shape is formed by the combination of several arcs of various radii. The report emphasises the northwest-southeast line of symmetry, but when the postholes are highlighted, as in Figure 1, the symmetry, if any, appears to be around a line from the north-northeast to south-southwest, giving the ring a pear shape. This view of symmetry would ignore the central structure's rough alignment with the northwest gap in the ring. The intervals between the postholes varied between 0.5 and 1.8 metres, except as previously mentioned, at the northwest where there was a single gap of 2.8 metres. In the centre of the ring was a rectangular pattern of holes measuring 5 metres by 2 metres

Figure I

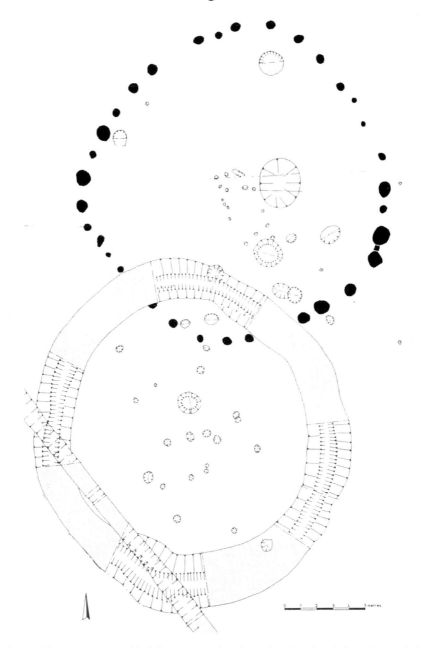

The Flixton Neolithic post hole circle in black, with the
later Bronze Age ring ditch.

*Adapted from RMC Atlas Aggregates Ltd. quarry Flixton Park Archaeolgical Excavations
and Monitoring Archive FLNO13 NO. 97/53 in Lowestoft Record Office*

with its long axis roughly in line with the northwest opening in the outer ring. The postholes were zoned according to their sizes, (see Figure 1) and nearly two kilograms of Neolithic grooved ware pottery, with its decorated side uppermost, had been placed in them. There was also worked flint, and heat altered material, with some possible human bones. The presence of an entrance suggested that the posts formed an otherwise continuous barrier. All this, the investigators thought, might point to a ritual use of the site. Phosphate studies make it unlikely that the site was used for funery purposes or as an animal stockyard.[8] Patrick Taylor made astronomical studies on the site and found that a central posthole lines up with the centre of the northwest entrance, and the most northerly point at which the moon sets in the winter. What does all this mean? Nobody knows what function the structure may have served, but whatever function it may have had, its presence clearly shows that 4,500 years ago Flixton had an organised society. The archaeologists have, moreover, shown that this site has remained important for thousands of years.

About 250 metres southwest of this find was another random group of 188 pits and postholes.[9] In these pits were 32 Neolithic artefacts mostly sherds of grooved ware, but also worked flints, centrally placed in the pits as if deliberately. There were 59 Iron Age pottery finds, the majority coming from only two of the pits. No remnants of Iron Age round houses were found. The report's conclusion was that 'on balance the Iron Age archaeology must be considered to be domestic' and 'it is possible that in a widely dispersed unenclosed settlement other buildings lie beyond the excavated area.' Further excavations continue to reveal more of the archaeology as the quarrying process continues to destroy the site.

All the arable land in South Elmham has been field walked, and the results published in The Proceedings of The Suffolk Institute of Archaeology and History.[10] The Neolithic finds are shown on Map IV. In St. Peter a flint Neolithic arrowhead, a core made from a flint quern, and some waste flakes were found near the Beck at the western end of the parish. In St. Cross they found a Neolithic axe from the southern end, and two groups of similarly dated flintwork from the west of the parish. In St. James, Neolithic flintwork was found at the southern end of the old Greshaw Green. Other recorded finds include scatters of burnt flints, some of which may have an ancient origin. These Neolithic finds are sparse when compared with finds in Breckland, and on the sandlings. Whether these differences are due to the heaviness of the soil and the agricultural use of it, or indicate a real difference in Neolithic activity must be uncertain.

A further invitation for speculation comes from the curvilinear and parallel arrangement of field boundaries and tracks in both South Elmham and the neighbouring Ilketshall parishes. These run in a southeast northwest direction and are thus roughly at right angles to the river Waveney. (See Map II) I have reviewed all the early aerial photographs of South Elmham in the Cambridge archive of Aerial Photography, and coaxial patterns are not as obvious as the map suggests. The best is probably the view of All Saints church shown in Plate XXVIII. These linear patterns have been likened to the low stony banks called reaves on Dartmoor. These reaves are datable to the Bronze Age by examination of associated ruined buildings.[11] Neolithic evidence for this coaxial form of field boundary has been found beneath peat bogs in Ireland, and evidence for lowland reave systems have been found in Nottinghamshire and Berkshire.[12] Could what we see in South Elmham be more than 4000 years old? Does this mean that these heavy soils were cultivated, or at least cleared, at that time? Coaxial systems are also found adjoining the Waveney valley at Yaxley, and to the north of the river Gipping at Haughley.* An extensive area of coaxial field boundaries lies to the north of Diss in Norfolk. This area has a well defined northern edge that runs along a watershed that also defines the hundred and parish boundaries.[13] In all of these sites, the orientation of the coaxes seem to be influenced by the rivers, with a tendency to run at right angles to them. Edward Martin writes that, even a late Iron Age date for these fields would be too early, when one takes into account the sparse evidence for such early settlement in these areas.[14] Yet two Roman roads can be seen to cut through the coaxial field systems, the Pye road at Yaxley, and Margary 35 at Fressingfield, and strongly suggest that these field systems have a pre-Roman date. The Roman Stone Street in Ilketshall is straight in its southern third where it seems to cut through the field pattern to the west of it. To the north the road adopts a gently curving line mimicking the obvious coaxial field systems either side of it as though the Romans had adopted a pre-existing Iron Age track.

Most of these findings argue strongly for a pre Roman date for all these field systems. There were 2700 years between the beginning of the Bronze Age and the end of the Iron Age, time enough for the area to have been cleared again and again, in spite of the heaviness of the land, and the difficulties of removing the great trees. Bad weather and episodic disease is likely to have led to repeated dereliction and reclamation of the farmed

---

*The topic of coaxial systems is most recently reviewed in "Suffolk in the Iron Age" by Edward Martin in Land of the Iceni, The Iron Age in Northern East Anglia. Ed. John Davies and Tom Williamson. University of East Anglia. 1999.

Map II

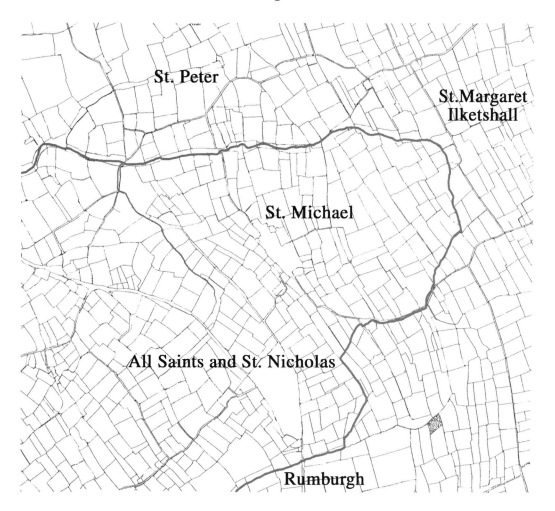

St. Peter

St.Margaret
Ilketshall

St. Michael

All Saints and St. Nicholas

Rumburgh

Ancient curvilinear field patterns in South Elmham

*Based on 1905 6 inch Ordnance Survey sheet 17
in Lowestoft Record Office*

land, yet there may have been retention of the old boundaries and tracks, or of their general direction. Looking at maps of these systems, it is easy to imagine that family groups in possession of land in the river valleys could have freely extended their holdings into the higher heavier and less desirable land, the only restriction being adjacent land holders with the same objective. Each group would develop their own patch, and no doubt some would become more dominant than others, and some tracks would become more important and longer than others.

I see the coaxial system not in any way as a planned landscape but as an evolution of land development from the river valleys by competing adjacent family groups in a time before kingship, when there was freedom to take whatever land could be used. It is surely of interest that this, the largest coaxial system in Suffolk is centred on the Neolithic posthole circle. In the Neolithic and early Bronze Age, the only certain routes in this fairly featureless and forested landscape would have been along the river valleys. Intrusions into the higher ground either side would surely have been tentative and gradual, and the development of well-marked ways would have been important. In the Neolithic era the wooden circle, and later, in the Bronze Age, the three barrows, standing high on the Flixton gravel terrace, could have acted as a markers for one of the routes onto the higher land. What might now be the remains of this route are suggested by the parish boundaries, and the ancient track called Uncle's Lane.

In those parts that remained untamed woodland, the predominant species were lime, hazel, oak, and elm, for these are the indications from pollen studies on Bronze Age deposits. Among the larger mammals there would have been red deer, roe deer, wolves, and possibly the last of the aurochs, ancient European cattle depicted so well in cave paintings in France. Beavers certainly existed in Britain but, if most of the woodland had been cleared from the river valleys, their habitat would have gone from South Elmham. There were no rabbits, no fallow deer, no rats or pheasants.

Some rare evidence of Bronze Age domestic life has been found near Mildenhall at West Row with postholes of round houses 5 metres in diameter, with porches protecting their entrances.[15] With them was evidence that they kept cattle, sheep, goats, pigs, horses, and dogs, and that they grew wheat, barley, and flax. The evidence for Bronze Age metalwork in South Elmham lies with the discovery of a bronze axe head of about 1300 BC in All Saints. (See Plate II) This was found by J. Woodrow and is now in the Beccles Museum. But the main evidence for this era of mankind's activity is in the four "ring ditches" on the gravel terrace in Flixton. The one that lay on the Neolithic site was a slightly irregular circle with an internal diameter of 15 metres and an external of 20 metres. (See Figure I) Just east of the centre was the cremation pit filled with charcoal rich sand and many obvious bone fragments, and burnt flints. The charcoal was almost entirely oak, with a little ash, with a carbon date of 3810-3624 BP (Before Present). There were 18 postholes in a cluster around the cremation site. Two hundred and fifty metres to the north was another 'ring ditch'. This ditch was spotted at the quarry face, and subsequently shown to be 4.7m wide and 1.69m deep, with a diameter of 40m. There was still a mound, but this was not at its centre. A cremation burial with its early Bronze Age pottery was found also eccentrically placed, and not under the mound. Two metres to the south-southwest of this was a Saxon inhumation grave with an east-west orientation. The acid soil had left only a faint skeletal trace, but enough to show that the skull lay at the west end. Near the neck of the body were two bronze brooches, but beside the head was a much more important find. It was the crushed fragments of a green glass claw beaker, only 59 of which have been found in Britain, one of these at the high status Snape ship burial[16]. This, the two brooches and some scattered pottery fragments date from the sixth century AD. Further Saxon burials, to the north and south west of the barrow, were suggested by the detection of a fifth century bronze brooch, a sixth century bronze buckle, and two perforated fourth century Roman coins. The mound itself formed the base of a medieval windmill perhaps dating from the late 15th to early 16th century, for beside it was found a bronze scabbard tip typical of this time.[17]

Archaeological study of the Flixton Quarry site has revealed its prolonged importance as a place of ceremony and reverence for the dead. This stretched from 2470 BC to 600 AD, more than 3000 years. The continuity of its use is open to speculation. As a site for burial it must always have been for a chosen few, and one at least of these was honoured by having the rare green clawed glass beaker placed beside the head. Dymond and Northeast have noted that on the Felixstowe peninsula, round barrows are on, or very near to parish boundaries, and that this is also found in Breckland. They suggest that these boundaries may have been in existence since the second or first millennium BC.[18] In Flixton the ring ditch numbered FLN 013 in the archaeological report lies only a few metres from the Flixton-Homersfield boundary[7]. Perhaps this too suggests an ancient boundary, which here runs so truly at right angles to the river Waveney, and unlike any of the other local riverside boundaries, is opposite and coincident with a Norfolk boundary dividing Earsham from Denton. Not only this, but looking south, it is clear that the line of this boundary continues, at first dividing Flixton from St. Margaret, then St. Peter from St. Margaret, and finally, as it joins the line of the ancient track called Uncle's Lane, it divides St. Michael from All Saints. The line of this ancient track continues across the Beck into the northern part of Rumburgh as far as the watershed between the Waveney and the Blyth, where the Buck Inn now stands.

The first use of iron in Britain was in about 700 BC and it was soon after this that the Greeks and Romans began writing about the barbarians to the North of them. This literacy spread through Europe[19] but it was not until Caesar's exploits in Britain in 54 BC that we learn of the names of the Celtic tribes of the East. The tribe living in what is now South Elmham were the Iceni, and to the South of them were the Trinovantes. The Iceni were among the five tribes submitting to Caesar at that time, but their origins are unknown. The Trinovantes made wheel thrown pottery showing Belgic influence, whereas the Iceni did not use the wheel and had their own designs. This suggests a long and local tradition of pottery making, and therefore a longer tribal history in the region.[20] Pagan Celtic religion was well developed, and complex, and is revealed in their artefacts, but none of these have been found in South Elmham.

Plate IV

An early Iceni Coin found in South Elmham
Photographed by Mr. J. Woodrow
By kind permission of the Curator of Beccles Museum

From the last Ice Age to the earliest evidence of human activity

The archaeological evidence for Celtic activity in S. Elmham rests with the finds of Iron Age sherds in most of the parishes, [10] and as we have seen there was evidence of probable domestic activity in Flixton. Further evidence for another settlement was found during the excavation of a new pond behind Rookery Farm in St. Margaret. Here there were a few postholes and a pit containing flint gritted Iron Age pottery. (See Plate III) One early Iceni coin was found in the district by Mr. James Woodrow, and is now in the Beccles Museum. (See Plate IV) On one side is shown the standard though varying image of a horse, and on the other a pattern. Either a head or a boar could at times replace this pattern. These variations do not help in identifying the exact origin of the coins.

The 700 years of Iron Age local history are almost totally unknown to us, yet we do know that right at the end of this the Iceni had a powerful leader and must have had a competent weapon making industry, and other warlike tools, and chariot making experts. Were the 700 years uneventful? Certainly not! In the early years of the 1st century AD, conflict between the various Celtic tribes was intense. There was a war between the Catuvellauni under their king Cunobelin, (Shakespeare's Cymbeline) and the Iceni, during which the Iceni were pushed back from their strongholds in Suffolk, and Cambridgeshire, as far north as Thetford. It was the death of Cunobelin and the subsequent dispute over his succession that saved the Iceni from defeat. The Roman knowledge of this dispute, and the presence of the dispossessed pro-Roman king Verica, or Berica, encouraged the Claudian invasion of Britain in 43 AD. What influence these events had on the inhabitants of South Elmham is not known. Almost certainly the men, and possibly the women also, would have been involved in fighting against Cunobelin, but the district probably remained in the hands of the Iceni.

Iron would have had another very important use on the heavy soils of our district, in the production of ploughshares. None have been found locally, but evidence that they were in use is shown by the plough that was found at an Iron Age temple at Frilford in Berkshire.[21] The most important Celtic archaeological finds in Suffolk are concentrated in the Sandlings, and in Breckland. The six golden torcs found at Ipswich (the richest Iron Age find in England) reflect the wealth of these districts. Peter Warner contrasts the slow lane of poverty, security, and boredom in the clay lands with the fast lane of insecurity, riches, and excitement of the Sandlings and Breckland in the Iron Age.[22] He may be right, the Iron Age certainly saw the beginning of the recording of named tribes, and their conflicts, power and wealth. These were troubled times. Before them, cooperative groups may have been defending themselves against nothing but the harshness of Nature, and in doing so, forming the coaxial field and track systems in South Elmham and at other sites in East Anglia. Ahead lay the trauma of Roman conquest and occupation.

[1] Moorlock B.S.P. et al in 'The Geology of the Countryside Around Lowestoft and Saxmundham' British Geological Survey London. The Stationary Office (2000) p.74

[2] Coxon, quoted by Moorlock et al in 'The Geology of the Country around Lowestoft and Saxmundham'. British Geological Survey. Stationary Office. (2000) p.70

[3] Ibid. p. 70.

[4] Ibid. p. 70.

[5] P.E.J.Wiltshire, and P.L.Murphy. 'Current Knowledge of the Iron Age Environment and Agrarian Economy of Norfolk and Adjacent Areas'. *Land Of The Iceni*. Ed. J. Davies and Tom Williamson.(1999) pp. 141-143

[6] Proceedings of The Suffolk Institute Of Archaeology and History Vol. 37. (1990) p. 268.

[7] RMC Atlas Aggregates Ltd. Quarry, Flixton Park, Flixton. Archive Report FLN 013 Report No. 97/53. Lowestoft Record Office.

[8] Ibid.

[9] Ibid. Reports No. 99/75, FLN 056 and FLN057.

[10] M.J.Hardy and E.A.Martin. Field Surveys. Proceedings of The Suffolk Institute of Archaeology and History. Volumes 36-37
St. Cross Vol. 36. pp. 147-9
St. James Vol. 36. pp. 149-50
St. Margaret Vol. 36. pp. 232-4
All Saints & St. Nicholas. Vol. 36. pp. 234-5
St. Michael & St. Peter. Vol. 36. pp. 315-7
Flixton Vol. 37. pp. 66-9

[11] Oliver Rackham. *The History of the Countryside*. Phoenix Giant. (1986) p.156

[12] Ibid. pp. 156-7

[13] Tom Williamson. *The Origins of Norfolk*. Manchester University Press. (1993) Figure 2.1

[14] *A Historical Atlas of Suffolk*. Suffolk County Council. (1999) p. 40

[15] Ibid. p. 38

[16] W. Filmer Sanker. *Snape Anglo-Saxon Cemetry*. in 'The Age of Sutton Hoo' Ed. M.O.H.Carver (1992) p. 42

[17] Martin, Pendleton, and Plouviez. Proceedings of The Suffolk Institute of Archaeology and History Vol. 37. (1990) p. 268

[18] David Dymond and Peter Northeast. *A History of Suffolk*. Darwen County History Series. Phillimore. (1995) p. 19

[19] Colin Renfrew. *Archaeology and Language*. Jonathan Cape. (1987) p.34

[20] Peter Warner. The Origins of Suffolk. Manchester University Press. (1996) p. 30

[21] Anne Ross. Pagan *Celtic Britain*. Sphere Books Ltd. (1974) p. 70

[22] Peter Warner. *Origins of Suffolk*. Manchester University Press. (1996) p. 28

Chapter II

The Roman Occupation

How did the 400 years of Roman occupation affect South Elmham? In general these 400 years left little other than roads.[1&2] The insensitive handling of the Celts in Eastern Britain, their consequent revolt, and their subsequent brutal suppression, may however have left its mark on South Elmham. Tacitus, in his Annals of Imperial Rome, writes that the king of the Iceni, Prasutagus, lived long and prosperously, and made his own two daughters co-heirs with the Roman Emperor. In so doing he had hoped by his submissiveness to preserve his kingdom from attack, but after his death his widow, Boudicca, was flogged and her daughters raped. The Icenian chiefs were deprived of their hereditary estates as if the Romans had been given the whole country. The king's relatives were treated like slaves. The Roman ex-soldiers to the South drove out the Trinovantes from their homes in Camulodunum (Colchester). Such was the provocation these two Celtic tribes endured, that they united in massive revolt against the occupying Roman forces in AD 60. They destroyed Camulodunum, then Londinium and Verulamium (St. Albans), before eventually being overcome with a great slaughter, somewhere along Watling Street. (According to Tacitus there were 80,000 Celts killed, and only 400 Romans.)[3] The subsequent Roman vengeance against the remainder of the tribes that had revolted, was a ruthless use of fire and sword, laying waste their territories. The surviving Celts were also distressed by starvation, for the Boudiccan army had left their fields unplanted, expecting to plunder Roman stores.[3] The Romans were anxious about eastern Britain, and it is likely that it was at this time that forts were built at Ixworth, Coddenham, and Chelmsford, with another larger headquarters at Great Chesterford in Essex. Perhaps Caister by Norwich was used to subdue the north of the region.[4] Roman camps would have been necessary in the suppression of the Iceni of the well populated Waveney valley. Tacitus writes that after the victory of Suetonius over the Boudiccan revolt, he reinforced the ninth legion with 2000 regular troops from Germany, 8 auxiliary infantry units, and 1000 cavalry. These were kept together under canvas in new winter quarters.[3] Surely, with so large an enterprise, there must have been other camps, as yet unconfirmed by archaeology, such as the earthwork that surrounds The Old Minster in South Elmham. It would be difficult to attribute this earthwork to any other era. It does not have the dominant position, nor the rounded form, of most Iron Age forts. There was a rectangular Iron Age enclosure at Gallow Hill Thetford, but like other rectangular Iron Age enclosures in Norfolk it had a single entrance and an area of only 0.25ha. (0.6 acre) and stood boldly high in a commanding position, (nothing now remains of it). [5]

The enclosed site of The Old Minster is rectangular and about 4 acres. It is surrounded by a vallum, the spoil from which has been thrown inwards to form a rampart. At its maximum the present distance from the bottom of the vallum to the top of the rampart is about 10 feet. There are three entrances placed in the North, South, and East ramparts respectively. (See figure II) At the time of the invasion of Britain in 43AD the Roman army had auxiliary units called *cohors peditata* and *cohors equitata*, the former were infantry units made up of six "centuries" of 80 men, the latter also had a contingent of 120 cavalrymen.[6] Perhaps one of these units was stationed at The Old Minster site. Holder goes on to describe a Trajanic fort at Gelligaer (in South Wales), which was probably designed for a cohors peditata. It had an area of 3.7 acres. The best-excavated fort of a cohors equitata is at Wallsend and is a 4-acre site. Both of these camps are rectangular with four entrances, one in each side. They catered for more permanent use having stone built internal buildings. The Old Minster site is likely to have been used only briefly, and the troops may have been under canvas as Tacitus says. He also tells us that after the brutal suppression by Suetonius, his successor, Turpilianus 'neither provoked the enemy nor was harassed by them, and thus gained the honourable name of peace for what was disgraceful inactivity'. Whether disgraceful or not, inactivity seems now to have been appropriate. Perhaps during this time the Romans were quietly camped in this site. Was it Turpilianus who decided to place this camp on such an obscure site, hoping that being unseen it would not provoke the local Iceni?

The impact of the Roman revenge on the followers of Boudicca must have been dire for them, but we have no record of the feelings of these oppressed Celts. A hundred years earlier however, the Essenes of Palestine did write of their experience of the Romans: 'By intention their only thought is to do evil, and in deceit and trickery they conduct themselves with all the peoples.'[7] It was deceit and trickery that led to the Boudiccan revolt, and in turn made the Romans in Britain wall their towns. They were outnumbered by the Britons 4 or 5 to one and must have felt threatened by them.[8] Yet Norman Davies concludes in his book 'The Isles' that *'the legacy of Roman Britain consisted of a few roads, a few ruins, a few genes, and as the sole substantial item, not itself Roman, Christianity.'* And so for South Elmham the construction of a Roman camp, hardly a Christianising event, was eventually to form the site for The Old Minster.

Nearly five centuries later the Irish monk St. Fursa at Burgh Castle, and the Northumbrian St. Cedd at Bradwell in Essex, two of the earliest Christians to arrive after Saint Felix the Burgundian, chose to set up their monasteries within the walls of Roman forts. There may well have been no competition for these sites, and they would have provided building material, as witnessed by the church built by St. Cedd that still stands at Bradwell. The possibility that the Saxon Christians also used the Roman site at South Elmham will be discussed later.

In 324 AD Constantine became emperor, and remained so until his death in 337. His powerful personality and the Christian conviction that he had after his victory over Maxentius at Milvian Bridge (over the Tiber in Rome) in 312, gave the empire a respite from constant wars. By 326 Britain was sending three bishops, with a priest and a deacon, to attend the council of Arles. These represented York, London, and Lincoln, or possibly Colchester.[9] It was Constantine who styled the Lords day as *'dies solis'* (Sunday), a name that Gibbon says 'could not offend the ears of his pagan subjects'.[10] Gibbon throws light on the state of the early Christians in the following three sentences: *'a sect of unwarlike plebeians, without leaders, without arms, without fortifications, must have encountered inevitable destruction in a rash and fruitless resistance to the masters of the Roman legions. But the Christians, when they deprecated the wrath of Diocletian, or solicited the favour of Constantine, could allege with truth and confidence, that they held the principle of passive obedience, and that, in the space of three centuries, their conduct had always been comfortable to their principles'.* Under Constantine, 1,800 bishops administered the church.[11] How did all this affect South Elmham? Did the hierarchy in this most devout and pure evangelism reach South Elmham? Oppression and poverty could have made the promise of salvation attractive. Christianity did come to late Roman Britain, but Roman churches in Britain are almost never found even in archaeological studies. One rare exception was found at Icklingham near Mildenhall in west Suffolk in 1976. It was in the form of a rectangular building with an associated apsidal structure that could have been a baptistry. There were also three leaden tanks, one of which had been found near to the small apsidal building, and had the chi-rho symbol of Christ on it.[12] This rarity of Roman churches may be because Christian worship was originally done in secret, and by the middle of the 4th C episcopal organisation was already in decline. It seems that little case can be made for the existence of a place of Christian worship in Roman South Elmham. It is much more likely that pagan activity continued on the Flixton gravel terrace, where archaeological studies continue to reveal Roman artefacts. The most recent excavations have found two Roman aisled timber buildings, two pottery kilns, and a four-posted structure that may have been a granary. Archaeomagnetic dating of the kiln linings suggest that one had last been fired at the end of the 1st century, and the other between the end of the 3rd century and the first half of the 5th century.[13]

Field walking in the Saints has revealed many sites of Roman activity, sometimes in paired positions on either side of streams. There were 8 sites in St. Cross, 3 in St. James, 5 in St. Michael and St. Peter, 7 in All Saints and St. Nicholas, and 3 in Flixton. (See Map V) None of these finds suggested the presence of a brick, or stone Roman villa. It is more likely that they are the relics of artefacts used by Romans, or Romano-Britons in timber buildings. The most extensive find has been to the south of Heavyland Wood in Flixton. Here, remains of roof, floor, and box (flue) tiles, with some kiln wasters, and possible kiln furniture, suggest a tile production site. Nene valley and Oxford pottery sherds indicate the site was active in the 3rd century.[14] In February 1959 removal of topsoil at the gravel pit in Homersfield revealed a blackened area that had some Romano-British sherds in it. (Grid Ref TM 28828529) On excavation there was a late 3rd or early 4th century pottery kiln. This kiln had been made in the natural sand of the site, it was 4ft 9ins in diameter narrowing to 4ft 6ins at the top, and was 2ft 3ins deep. Its 9-inch walls were made from baked clay. A furnace arch separated this chamber from the stoke hole, which was 9ft 6ins wide, and 10ft 6ins long, and within this was a pit in which the stoker would have stood. During the excavation various potsherds were found most of which seem to have been made in the kiln. These were 46.5% dish fragments, 32.5% rusticated type jars, 16.6% shouldered bowls, and 4.4% cordoned jars. There were also 2 fragments of Samian ware, and the base of a colour coated Rhenish beaker of not earlier than the end of the 2nd century AD. There was also a two pronged iron flesh hook, and a sawn off tine from a red deer antler, which may have been used in the decoration of the unfired pots.[15] In 1963 during quarrying at Homersfield near to this previously excavated Roman kiln, Mr. Burford found a mould of a face that would have been used to decorate pottery. This mould was 3 inches long and 2.5 inches wide, and was dated as 3rd to 4th century AD. It is now in the Ipswich Museum.[16]

Outside, and well to the east of South Elmham, the northern end of the Roman Stone Street takes its gently waving course to the north north-west towards the ancient crossing of the Waveney at Wainford. In this northern part it clearly follows the surrounding field pattern. To the south the road is absolutely straight. These two parts of Stone Street meet in Ilketshall St. Lawrence between the roads to Rumburgh and Redisham (See plate VIII). At this point the aerial photograph clearly shows how the field pattern, which the road had followed to the north, veers off to the east away from the straight southern part of Stone Street (see plate IX). At this point stands the watershed between the Hundred River to the east and the Waveney to the west, and to the south the head waters of the Blyth, a likely territorial meeting point and possible explanation for the change in road alignment.

At Ilketshall St. Lawrence, the church stands on a rectangular platform 250 yards to the East of the road, this platform may also be Roman.[17]

Plate V

Roman Coins of Vespasian AD 67-79, and Severus Alexander AD 222-235
Found in South Elmham
By kind permission of the Curator of Beccles Museum

An Enigma of Ancient Suffolk

A scattering of Roman coins has been found in South Elmham mostly by metal detectors. Some of these are on display in Beccles museum. One carries the head of Vespasian (69-79 AD) and another that of Severus Alexander (222-235 AD) (See Plate V) Other Roman metal finds are of bronze brooches from various sites. These too are in Beccles Museum. (See Plates VI and VII)

[1] Peter Salway. *Roman Britain*. In The Oxford History of England. (1991)
[2] Norman Davies. *The Isles*. Macmillan (1999)
[3] Tacitus *The Annals of Imperial Rome*. Penguin Classics (1996) p. 331
[4] Malcolm Todd. *Roman Britain 55 BC – AD 400*. Fontana Press. (1985) p. 94
[5] Peter Warner. *Origins of Suffolk*. Manchester University Press. (1996) p. 131
[6] P.A.Holder. *Roman Army in Britain*. Batsford (1982) p. 31
[7] *The Dead Sea Scrolls*. A new translation by M. Wise, M. Abegg, and
     E. Cook. Harper Collins. (1996) p. 117
[8] Norman Davies. The Isles. Macmillan. (1999) p. 139
[9] Peter Salway. Roman Britain. The Oxford History of England. (1991) p. 340
[10] Edward Gibbon. *Decline and Fall of The Roman Empire*. World Classics.
     (1903) Vol. 2 p. 329
[11] Ibid. Vol. 2 p. 358.
[12] West and Plouviez. East Anglian Archaeology. Report No. 3. (1976) pp. 63-126
[13] Proceedings of The Suffolk Institute of Archaeology and Histor (2002)
     Vol. XL pp.222-225
[14] Ibid. Mike Hardy, and Edward Martin. (1988)Vol. 37 p. 66
[15] Ibid. Smedley and Owles. (1959) Vol. 28 p.168
[16] Ibid. Smedley and Owles. (1965) Vol. 30 p. 210
[17] Norman Scarfe. *The Suffolk Landscape*. Alastair Press. (1987) p. 116

Map I

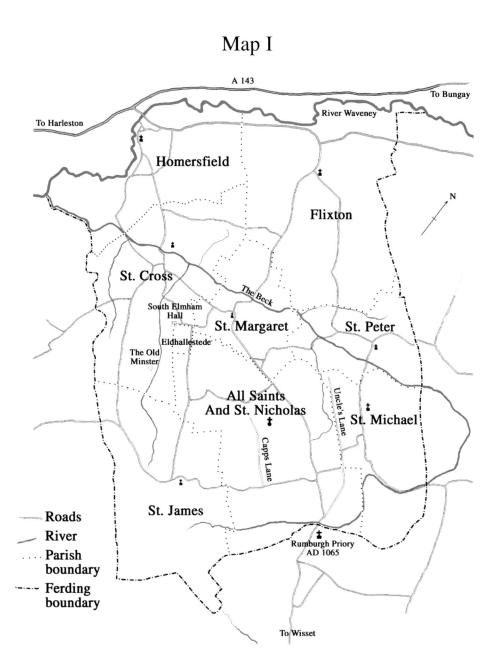

Map of South Elmham showing parish boundaries
Based on the Ordnance Survey sheet 156, 1974

Map III

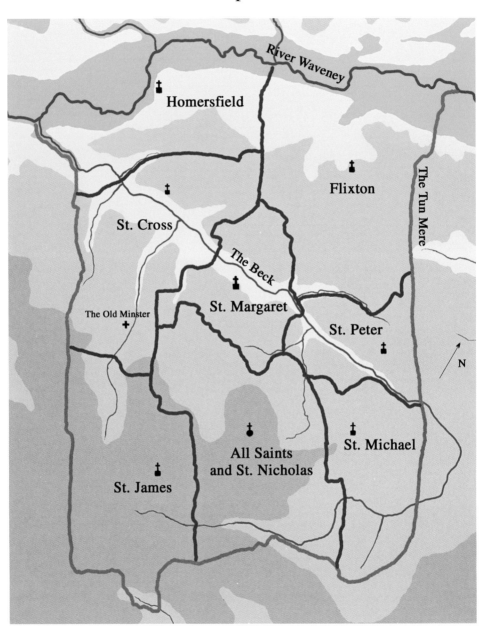

South Elmham's parish (blue) and ferding (red)
Boundaries, with contours, rivers and churches.

O <15 metres
O 15-30 metres
O 30-45 metres
O >45 metres

Map IV

River Waveney

Neolithic post hole
circle
3

The Beck
1

2

1

2

Stone Age Finds

1. Flint Tools
2. Struck Flints
3. Stone Age Grooved Ware

O <15 metres
O 15-30 metres
O 30-45 metres
O >45 metres

Map V

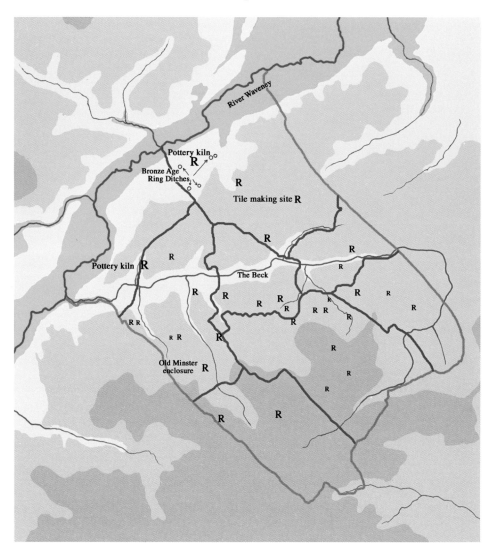

Pottery kiln

R

Bronze Age
Ring Ditches

R

Tile making site **R**

R

R

R

Pottery kiln **R**

R

The Beck

R

R

R **R**

R

R **R**

R **R**

R **R**

R

R

R R

R

R R

R

R

Old Minster
enclosure **R**

R

R

R

R

R

Map of the Roman Finds in South Elmham

With Parish and Ferding Boundaries

R = Roman finds. The larger the
letter the more important the find.

O <15 metres
O 15-30 metres
O 30-45 metres
O >45 metres

Plate II

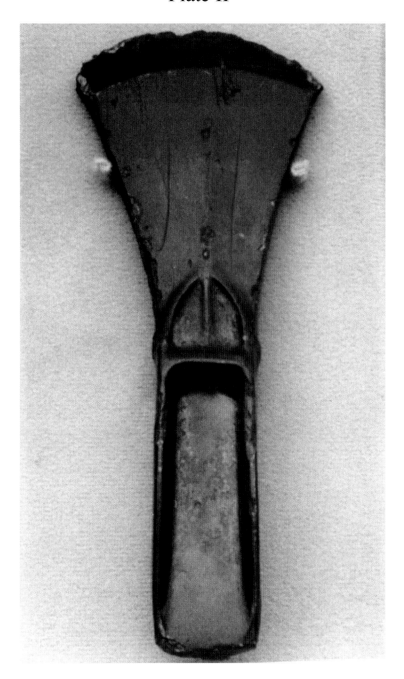

Bronze Age Axe Head. 1300BC
Length 9.25 inches. Found in South Elmham, now in Beccles Museum.
By kind permission of the Curator of Beccles Museum

Plate III

Flint Gritted Iron Age Pottery Sherds at Rookery Farm
By kind permission of Mrs. Wendy Walpole

Plate VI

A collection of Roman brooch fragments
Found in South Elmham, the largest measures 2.25 inches.
By kind permission of the Curator of Beccles Museum

Plate VII

One of the Roman brooches
shown in plate VI, in greater detail
Two and a quarter inches long.
By kind permission of the Curator of Beccles Museum

Chapter III

The Beginnings of Christianity in Saxon East Anglia

The spread of Christianity from St. Augustine's mission in Kent was like a flow of water spilled on the uneven ground of pagan society. It flowed in one direction only to dry up, and then flow elsewhere, then back again over the dry ground, eventually flooding the whole of England. East Anglia was early in this process, and although most of the action was distant from South Elmham itself, this story forms an important adjunct to the understanding of its ancient history. In concentrating on those parts of the story which are most relevent to South Elmham this account makes no mention of the great monastic foundations at Ely and Bury St.Edmunds or of the Saxon Saint Botolph, or King Anna and his saintly daughters.

St. Augustine's mission.

In 596 AD Pope Gregory sent the reluctant Augustine to preach to the English Nation. Augustine had been prior at the Pope's own monastery of St. Andrew in Rome, and must have been carefully chosen, for it is said that the pope himself had wanted to convert the English but had been prevented from leaving Rome by the inhabitants of that great city. After a long and anxious journey through Gaul, Augustine arrived on the Isle of Thanet with forty companions, including interpreters from among the Franks, some of whom he sent to King Ethelbert of Kent. After some days the King came to Thanet and sitting down in the open air, for he was afraid that magical arts could master him within a building, spoke with Augustine and his companions granting them a dwelling in Canterbury. Ethelbert's Queen Bertha was already a Christian from Gaul and was accustomed to using the old Roman church of St. Martin (in Canterbury) for prayer. It was in this church, the oldest church still in use today in England, that Augustine and his followers sang, prayed, preached, and baptised, eventually baptising Ethelbert himself. Bede (who is our best source for St. Augustine's life in England) then tells of great numbers gathering each day to hear the word of God.[1] At a visit to Arles, Augustine was consecrated archbishop of the English nation, and in AD 604 Augustine himself consecrated Mellitus bishop of the East Saxons in their capital of London, where they built a cathedral dedicated to St. Paul. In about 616 Augustine baptised King Raedwald of the East Angles, but Raedwald, Bede writes, was later persuaded to move away from the true faith by his wife and others, and tried to serve both Christ and the ancient gods. The making of adjacent Christian and pagan altars was no doubt outrageous to the Venerable Bede, but was nevertheless a first step for the new faith in East Anglia. Raedwald, however, left no bishop or other clerical establishment and was buried in an extravagantly pagan way in about 625 at Sutton Hoo, suggesting that his family and followers had rejected Christianity wholeheartedly.

A second chance to convert the kingdom came with the succession of Earpwald, Raedwald's son. Earpwald was baptised in about 627 AD, we do not know where or by whom, but it seems likely that Edwin, king of Northumbria had something to do with it, for William of Malmesbury[2] says that Edwin granted the empty title of king to Raedwald's son. (Empty because he was subservient to Edwin) Shortly afterwards Earpwald was murdered by a pagan called Rickbert, and so the province remained pagan for another year or so. In about 631 Earpwald's brother Sigebert, or perhaps he was his half brother on his mother's side, returned from exile in Gaul to become king.

King Sigebert and the Irish influence.

Sigebert was a man of learning and a devout Christian. He had been schooled in Gaul, and whereas Raedwald might have adopted Christianity for purely tactical reasons, Sigebert was deeply immersed in its divine teaching, and full of enthusiasm to copy what he had seen done so well in Gaul.[3] It was his succession that was so important in changing the outlook and organisation of the East Angles. Important, because he established a school for the education of boys in the study of letters, and fortunate in having Felix the Burgundian, who had been sent to East Anglia from Kent at his own request by Archbishop Honorius, to run the school, and to be his first bishop. [4] Felix was based at Domnoc, which Bede describes as a 'civitas' (or city). It is the site of Domnoc that has been the cause of much heated argument. Norman Scarfe in his discussion of place names suggests that the origin of the word may be the Celtic dubno meaning deep, perhaps used here to describe the deepness of the water at Dunwich.[5] Others have suggested that Domnoc was at Walton near Felixstowe, but Walton was a Roman Saxon Shore fort and should have been described as a 'castrum' by Bede, the word he used to describe Cnobheresburg (probably Burgh Castle). It is tempting to think that Felixstowe was named after Saint Felix and that the name indicates the proximity of his see. But Felixstowe does not appear in the Domesday Book and the earliest spelling of the word was Filchestou in 1254.[6] Wherever Domnoc was, there is another Celtic word that more aptly describes the site of the first church and see of the East Anglian Kingdom. This word was *'domnach,'* a name that had been associated with many of the churches that may have been founded by St. Patrick in Ireland. The Celtic scholar Elizabeth Rees describes *domnach* as a pre monastic word meaning church [7], derived from the Latin 'Dominus' meaning the Lord. She goes on to say that there are about thirty churches named Domnach Patraic scattered across Northern Ireland. The Irish influence was strong in Saxon East Anglia. Sigebert had honourably received the monk Fursa and his followers from Ireland, giving them Cnobheresburg where they established a monastery in AD 633. Could it be that Fursa and his followers, knowing the word *'domnach'* in Ireland, used it to name, or rename, the first place given to Felix for him to spread the Good Word? This of course gets us no nearer to knowing where it was, but may explain why the word is not a place name now.

Another Irish link involves Felix himself, and possibly Sigebert. An Irish monk named St. Columbanus, whose long life spanned the years between the mid 6th and 7th centuries, set sail as a young man from Ireland on his peregrination hoping to reach Gaul. He was successful, and travelled across land with his twelve companions to the upper reaches of the river Saone. Here he met another King Sigibert who 'ruled with honour' the kingdom of Austrasia. Sigibert granted him freedom to choose a hermitage, and Columbanus chose a desolate ruined castle in the Vosges Mountains. Here, after great privation, he established his first monastery, and much later, as his following increased, he made another foundation in a fortified site at Luxeuil, and later still at Fonataines. These became important seats of learning, and so the teaching of Columbanus and the order that he established became, at least for a few decades, influential. The life of this great man, written shortly after his death by a monk called Jonas, is full of events and miraculous achievements. Columbanus comes across as a man of learning and leadership, and in spite of the privations he imposed on himself, a man of good humour.[8] He would have been amazed to know that, in December 2002, Pope John Paul decreed that he be made the patron saint of motorcyclists.[9]

What relevance has this to St. Felix and to our King Sigebert? Felix is always referred to as the Burgundian, and if this is true, then it is highly likely that he was a brother in one of the monasteries set up by Columbanus. It is likely that Columbanus and Felix never met, Columbanus having left before Felix joined his order. It is also possible that Sigebert was there. We will probably never know these things, but Bede's comment that Felix went to East Anglia by his own desire, encourages one to think that he may have already met Sigebert in Burgundy. If there is any truth in these ideas it would give the East Anglian Church a strong Irish flavour, and more than this it would give poignancy to the way Bede describes Felix as running his school in accordance with the practice of Canterbury, suggesting that he might otherwise have run it with a Celtic bias.[3] It also adds strength to the possibility that the name *Dommoc* or *Domnoc* that Bede gives to the first site of the bishopric of the East Angles has its origin in the Irish Celtic word *Domnach*.

Fursa was an Irish nobleman, and Bede describes him as even more noble in mind than in birth. It was these intellectual and spiritual qualities, and his three visions, some of the first recorded visions of hell, that made him famous and revered. Inspired by the goodness of his teaching Bede tells us that many unbelievers were converted, but just as Fursa had shunned the crowds in Ireland for a peregrination to England, so he found the worldly business of running the monastery in Cnobheresburg irksome[10]. Therefore he freed himself from this, and joined his brother Ultan, who after many years of monastic life had become a hermit. They lived together for a year in prayer, austerity, and manual labour. Bede's account does not state where this was, but there is an inference in his text that it was in the 'province of the East Angles'. Nobody knows where this was, but there was a strong tradition for using old Roman sites for new Christian purposes, as we think Fursa did at Burgh Castle. Richard Morris gives many instances of forts being used for Christian purposes.[11] Prince Maelgwyn Gwynedd gave the fort at Holyhead to a 6th century Cornish holy man called Cybi; in 653 AD St. Cedd had royal encouragement to set up his mission at the old Roman fort of Othona at Bradwell in Essex. King Egbert gave the Roman fort at Reculver in Kent to Bassa the priest. Another royal gift was of the Roman fort at Ebchester in Northumberland, and a much earlier example is of St. Sampson, a 5th century monk who left his monastery at Lantwit Major and withdrew to an old fort near Cardiff before going on to Brittany. As we have seen above, Columbanus used two old fortified sites in Gaul for his monasteries. Most of these grants of land were made between 630 and 700 AD and one can contemplate the possibility that Fursa and Ultan came to the Roman site in St. Cross as hermits, and in doing so gave the place its feeling of holiness, mystery, and peace.

After this year of solitude with his brother, Fursa sailed to Gaul where he founded a monastery at Lagny on the river Marne. He had left his monastery at Cnobheresburg in the hands of his brother Foillan and the priests Gobban and Dicul. Bede says he left because he thought that the heathen raids were a danger even to the monasteries, and within a year or so, the heathen Mercians had overrun the monastery at Cnobheresburg. Foillan had escaped to Gaul, and was later followed by Ultan, where both became venerated as Saints, Foillan eventually having the great church adjacent to Charlemagne's palace dedicated to him, where even now there is a 15th century figure of him protected by an iron grill near the altar. Ultan became abbot of Fosses and of Peronne. Dicul it is thought may have given his name to Dickleburgh in Norfolk. This priest should not be confused with the Irish monk Dicul who went to the pagan province of the South Saxons and set up a small monastery at Bosham near Chichester. Here, with five or six brothers, the local pagans ignored his preaching.[12] (If, by any chance, this was the same man he would have been very old, for it must have been about 50 years after the founding of the monastery at Cnobheresburg.)

The establishment of the diocese of Elmham.

At the synod of Hertford in AD 673 the diocese of East Anglia was divided into two parts, and two bishops were appointed to do the work of the ailing bishop Bisi. No mention is made in Bede's text of the title of the second see, though he names its first bishop as Badwine. It is clear however, from the 12th century writings of William of Malmesbury, and attendance records at subsequent synods and other meetings that it was named Elmham.

Why did they choose Elmham, and which Elmham? Two 19th century historians Suckling[13] and Copinger[14] wrote that King Sigebert gave the land that we now call South Elmham to his bishop Felix. They give no evidence for this, and the more cautious Reverend Raven did not mention it in his 'History of Suffolk' 1895. Nevertheless, it was common practice for such regal gifts to be made both for monastic and secular religious foundations, and Sigebert did give land at Cnobheresburg (probably Burgh Castle) to Fursa.[10]

South Elmham is unique in its ancient administrative structure. Its three Domesday parishes (Flixton, Homersfield, and Elmham,) formed a 'ferding' or fourth part of the hundred of Wangford. How far the hundredal system goes back in time is not clear, but by the early 11th century it was a well-organised method of collection of taxes, and administration of justice. Hundred courts would have been held in the open at Wainford, the Waveney crossing just downstream from Bungay. The description of South Elmham as a ferding suggests that it had a separate administrative arrangement. This becomes clear from evidence in the ancient records of the 'Norwich Taxation of 1254' which describes an ecclesiastical system of deacons and archdeacons collecting taxes for Pope Nicholas. In Suffolk there was an archdeacon for Sudbury, and another for Suffolk. Each deacon was responsible for a deanery. In the 14 deaneries under the control of the Suffolk archdeacon, all except three were named after their hundred, and the areas were defined by the hundred boundaries. South Elmham was one of these deaneries, and was distinct from Wangford, and unique in not being a whole hundred. This system of deaneries followed William the Conqueror's rule that civil and ecclesiastical jurisdiction should be separated, so that no bishop or archdeacon would hold pleas in a hundred court, nor bring a cause that relates to the rule of souls to the judgement of secular men.[15]

Although the system of deaneries was a post Conquest innovation, the post of deacon was much older, as shown by their attestations on 9th century charters. The word, derived from decanus, referred to the head of a group of ten secular, as opposed to monastic, clergy.[16] If such a group existed in Saxon South Elmham they would have had a 'minster' as their base. It is possible that we know the name of one of the deacons of Elmham. This was a man called Hunferth, described as diaconus or deacon, who in 803 AD accompanied bishop Alhheard of Elmham on his visit to the synod at Clofeshoh. (See page 44) In contrast to this, North Elmham though a large parish, formed only a small part of the Deanery of Brisely that included the whole hundred of Launditch.

Minster and Old Minster.

The word minster is the Old English form of the Latin monasterium meaning monastery. The word has however been used in various contexts. For example the Canterbury Manuscript of the Anglo-Saxon Chronicles for 903 AD reports 'Here Grimbald the priest passed away, and in this year the New Minster in Winchester was consecrated' This New Minster was the West Saxon Cathedral. On the other hand, a code of King Edgar issued at Andover in 959 AD directs that all payment of tithe is to be made to the old minster to which the parish belongs. In a law code issued by Aethelred in 1008 a minster could mean a regular monastery, or a church with a community of canons. Aethelred's code of 1014 describes three kinds of minster, a head minster or cathedral, a medemdran or old minster, and those of even less importance. This last category was usually in private ownership, some would have a graveyard, but those without were referred to as fieldkirken. This last, privately owned category, presumably became the parish churches.[17] John Blair points out how little we know about minster churches. He says that between the mid 7th and the mid 9th centuries hundreds of them were founded, and that they formed important local centres for religious activity and thus the basis for the parochial system.[18] It was these buildings that were referred to in late Saxon times as old minsters. Their large area of influence later became divided into the parishes we now have. In time parish churches, which had developed from the private manorial churches, made the minster redundant. Some minsters became large parish churches themselves, (like Bampton in Oxfordshire[18]) others may have retained a monastic function, and some, like The Old Minster South Elmham, may have been abandoned.

This is a particularly attractive explanation for the use of the term old minster to describe the ruin in St. Cross. It would also explain the redundancy of the building, which would have developed as each of the nine parishes established its own church and priest. Somewhat against this theory is Ridgard's review of the 14th century 'Account Rolls of South Elmham Manor'. In these the term 'old minster' is never used, only 'le Menstre', 'le Mynstre', or the Latin Monasterium.[19] Whether this was an important indicator of function in South Elmham is impossible to know. It may be that it had a dual role of being a monastery and an old minster. It has been suggested by Peter Warner that South Elmham might have been at the centre of three minster lands.[20] To the west lay Mendham, where Theodred (Bishop of London) mentioned the existence of a minster in his will of about 960 AD.[21] To the east, Ilketshall, may have had Bungay as its organising centre,[22] and could have been the third minster land.

North Elmham.

North Elmham, like South Elmham, has good evidence of Neolithic, Bronze Age, and Iron Age activity. What distinguishes North Elmham is its vast 5th–6th century Anglo-Saxon cremation cemetery at Spong Hill. This is so large that it undoubtedly served as a burial ground for much more than the local community, and must have been an important pre-Christian site.[23] A 7th century Middle Saxon settlement was established well away from Spong Hill over a mile to the northwest on new ground. The results of excavations in this Old Park area have shown a complexity of Saxon foundations dating from the mid 7th century to the end of the 11th[24] One large L shaped building could possibly have been a 10th century bishop's palace. One hundred and eighty six inhumation burials, of middle Saxon date, were found on this same site.[25] Adjacent to the Old Park is the ruin of what most authorities consider to have been the Cathedral, though in its present form is probably the church rebuilt by the first bishop of Norwich,

Herbert de Losinga at the end of the 11th century as his own chapel, and later converted by bishop Herbert Despenser as his fortified manor house.[26] Beneath this building, excavation has shown the remains of three previous timber buildings, but no evidence of a Cathedral before the Danish incursions of the mid 9th century.[27]

Perhaps in confirmation of the importance of these timber buildings is the 13th century First Register of Norwich Cathedral Priory, [28] though it is by no means a contemporary record, it refers to the bishop's wandering seat, at one time, at a wooden chapel in a village called Elmham, and at another, at the little town of Thetford. Here we have an early reference to a wooden chapel at Elmham, which may well be referring to the wooden foundations found at North Elmham.

The Domesday Book records 6 churches in the Suffolk Elmham and only one in the Norfolk Elmham. (See Tables I, II, III, and XII) The only church at North Elmham had a glebe of 60 acres and 1 plough, valued at 5s and 4d, and was part of the bishop's manor of 8 carucates worth a total of £10, whereas the best endowed of the 6 South Elmham churches had 40 acres and $1/2$ a plough and was part of the bishop's estate of 2 carucates 20 acres with a total value of £4. (A carucate may have been about 120 acres) There is no indication of which South Elmham church this was, except that it was in Elmham, and not in Flixton that had one church, or Homersfield, that had two churches.

It was the bishop of Thetford that held both these large estates and their churches after 1070. Before 1066 Aelmer, the bishop of Elmham, held Elmham in Norfolk, and most of the ferding of Elmham in Suffolk. Nearly all the rest belonged to his brother Stigand the archbishop of Canterbury. No mention is made of the see in either the Norfolk or Suffolk Elmham in The Domesday Book, a strange omission because there is little doubt that in 1066 the see was at North Elmham. It seems even more surprising when one looks at the entry for Hoxne in the Bishop's Hundred which is as follows; *'In this manor is a church, the Episcopal see of Suffolk before 1066'*. By 1086 (when the Domesday Book had been completed) the single bishopric for the whole of East Anglia had moved from North Elmham to Thetford.

Is there any more information on the see of Elmham?

There is no contemporary written evidence that indicates the original sites of either the first or the second East Anglian sees with any certainty. As we have seen above, it had generally been assumed that King Sigebert had given South Elmham to his first bishop Felix, and that this accounts for the name of the parish of Flixton. There is certainly no evidence of any such nominal links in North Elmham. Some have commented on the proximity of South Elmham to the original East Anglian see, assuming this to have been at Dunwich, and for this reason have felt that North Elmham would be, at least administratively, a much more likely site. The Reverend J.J.Raven wrote in 1895 'It may be that the establishment of a see at South Elmham was all that was at that time possible, while the tide of paganism, so late at the flood, was slowly ebbing from the borderland of the Waveney valley'.[29] This concept is supported by the recent discovery of evidence for probable cult activity on the gravel beds beside the Waveney in Flixton that may have persisted well into the Saxon era. Any attempt to set up a see north of the Waveney would have been dependant on the agreement of the local leaders, who, though they might have supported the king in battle, may well have refused baptism. The benefits of leaving a high ranking member of the royal family unbaptised to represent a pagan faction may sometimes have helped to unite a kingdom, and at others contributed to its division.[30] The process of Christianisation of a kingdom was not without its problems. However, at the time of the formation of the see of Elmham in 673 AD Aldwulf, a Christian, was king of the East Angles, owing allegiance to Penda's son Wulfhere, the king of Mercia, also a Christian. There is nothing else to help us to understand the religious outlook of the local leaders in the region of what is now North Elmham at this time.

Where is the evidence for early occupation of The Old Minster site? Suckling, in his History of Suffolk of 1846, tells us that George Durrant, the occupier of South Elmham Hall in the 1840's, had the whole interior of the Minster dug to a depth of five feet and found nothing, except a few bones, and a small piece of old iron, with one or two ancient keys. He also writes that '*the frequent discovery by the plough, of urns filled with burnt bones and ashes, seems to confirm the voice of tradition very current in the village, that the Minster occupies the site of a pagan temple.*'[31] It is generally assumed that Suckling is quoting the Lowestoft historian Gillingwater, who visited the site in 1804 when the whole enclosure had recently been dug by spade or by plough. He implied that substantial numbers of broken fragments of urns containing 'calcined' ashes were uncovered. The Lowestoft Record Office has several fragments of paper on which Mr. Gillingwater has written about a visit he made to the site on June the 9th 1804. One of these was as follows:

'*On June 9th 1804 I visited the ruin of that ancient structure in St. Margarets South Elmham called the Old Minster. This building is situated not far from the centre of a parallelogram whose sides are about …………. and which still continues to be enclosed by a Moat running on every side of it, and a mound of earth, which appears to have been cast out of the Moat when first made. The area of this parallelogram (now arable land) was without doubt made use of originally as a burial place for such people as were in any manner connected with the building as is evident from the numerous pieces of urns frequently discovered in this place by the spade or the plough, and whose interior parts are blackened with the calcined ashes of human bodies that were contained therein.*'[32]   None of these urns has survived for us to see, and it is not clear from these notes whether Gillingwater saw any himself, in fact it rather suggests that he did not. In the 1940's, workmen on a road near to Beccles found some Saxon cremation jars that surely must be similar to those that Gillingwater was describing. These are now in the Beccles museum (See plate X).

Whatever the truth of this matter is, very little has been found on subsequent digs to suggest that the site was an important pagan or Christian burial ground, except for the find of a small piece of worked stone (ashlar) incorporated in the wall of the minster considered because of its interlace carving to be Saxon. This fragment must have come from the grave of an important person, perhaps one of the bishops of Elmham.

Why is there so little archaeological and written evidence for the bishopric of Elmham? The archaeological investigation of South Elmham is in its very early stages, and it is likely that much of the evidence still lies beneath the topsoil awaiting the finance and manpower for its discovery. In comparison with North Elmham the records of archaeological investigations in South Elmham are few, the disparity being due in part to the less disturbed and archaeologically more inviting landscape at North Elmham. The relative absence of findings at South Elmham should not necessarily be construed as meaning the absence of important Anglo-Saxon activity there.

The meagre written evidence tells us that the bishopric was established at the synod of Hertford in AD 673, and of the succession of bishops at intervals of four to thirty five years until Hunberht was consecrated in 824 AD. The best review of the names and dates of consecration of the bishops of Elmham before the Danish incursion is that of Dorothy Whitelock.[33] After the death of Hunberht probably in 869 there was a sinister interval of 86 years until his successor Eadulf. The sequence of bishops of Elmham was as follows:

AD 673 Beaduwine
     706 Nothberht
     731 Heathulac
     736 Aethelfrith
     742 Eanfrith
     781 Aethelwulf
     785 Alhheard
     814 Sibba
     816? Hunferth
     824 Hunberht
     955 Eadulf - *Probably the first appointment to North Elmham*

The first Danish raids were in Northumbria in 793 when the great monastic settlement on Lindisfarne was sacked. By 835 AD Danish armies were over wintering in England, and in 841 great destruction was done in East Anglia. Again in 865 as Sir Frank Stenton explains *'the whole fabric of English society was threatened by a great army which landed in East Anglia prepared to spend many consecutive years in deliberate exploitation of all the opportunities for profit which England offered.'*[34] The first year of Danish occupation was spent securing horses and raiding the local countryside. After a foray into Yorkshire the Danes returned to settle in Thetford. In 869 AD, they fought, defeated, and killed King Edmund. The Anglo Saxon Chronicle entry for the year 870 is *'Edmund the King fought against them, and the Danes took the victory, killing the King, and overcame the land. They destroyed all the churches they came to; the same time they took Peterborough, they burned and broke, killed the abbot and monks, and all they found there. They made that which was very great such that it became nothing.'* What chance was there that anything would have survived this at South Elmham? Thus warfare has always been both destroyer, and creator, of history. Bishop Hunberht of Elmham could have been slain in the earlier Danish raids, (his last recorded attestation was in 845) and any remnant of organised Christian activity destroyed in these later raids. Simon of Durham wrote that bishop Hunberht shared Edmund's martyrdom in 869,[32] and Norman Scarfe thinks there may yet be a relic of bishop Hunberht concealed in the name of Homersfield.[35] (See Chapter IV)

Was the see at North or South Elmham?
    The controversy concerning the site of the second episcopal see of the East Angles established in 673 AD began in 1884. In this year a Norfolk

man Henry Harrod challenged the opinions of the great 16th, 17th, 18th and 19th century antiquarians and historians. The first of these, William Camden, was in no doubt that the two bishoprics were at Dunwich and North Elmham ('Britannia' 1586). Sir Henry Spelman in the 17th century, and Francis Blomfield in the mid 18th century concurred with this view, and neither did Alfred Suckling in his History of Suffolk of 1846 question it. But Henry Harrod argued strongly that South Elmham had been the site of the see.[36] He pointed out that Flixton derived its name from St. Felix and that the nine parishes formed a 'parochia' a term anciently applied, he said, to the site of a see. This had further confirmation by the unique persistence for East Anglia of the term minster in South Elmham. It seems that some of this controversy arose from misreading and elaboration of the ancient texts, but most by the misconception that the bishopric had always been at one or other of the Elmhams, and not at both.

Why are there two Elmhams? Elmham as a village name occurs nowhere else in England, though there are many other place names beginning with Elm such as: Elmbridge, Elmhurst, Elmscott, Elmstead, Elmswell, and Elmton. The two Elmhams have strong ecclesiastical connections, and it seems very likely that one was named after the other. In the same way that emigrants name their new settlements after the village or town whence they came, so the religious community that moved from the original Elmham to another place might have wanted to carry with them the hallowed name of their ancient bishopric. There is little doubt that the bishopric in the late Saxon period was at North Elmham, and therefore that North Elmham was the second village with that name. Why did they choose North Elmham? South Elmham was obviously too close to the 10th century see at Hoxne and was not well placed to minister to Norfolk. The Launditch Hundred that included North Elmham was probably at the centre of a patch of the limited holdings of the secular (as opposed to the monastic) church in Norfolk. These holdings were limited in comparison to the vast estates of the great abbeys of Ely and Bury St. Edmunds. Perhaps the choice was in this way made easy, North Elmham also had the tradition of its ancient Saxon burial ground and was a thriving village in the middle and later Saxon times.

If one Elmham was named after the other then the first Elmham must have been in Suffolk. The names of its adjacent parishes of Flixton and Homersfield are testimony to their early ecclesiastical importance. No such nominal indicators of the pre-Danish church exist at North Elmham. More than this the archaeological evidence is against there being a pre-Danish church building at North Elmham.[37] Direct evidence for a pre-Danish church building in South Elmham is also lacking; but when one considers the undisturbed nature of the archaeology in the north, and the amount of time and effort spent on excavation there, it is no surprise that most of the archaeological literature concerns North Elmham, and therefore a negative finding in the north might carry more weight than the absence of findings in the south.

The Bishops of Elmham.

We know a little about the Bishops of Elmham from Anglo-Saxon charters. The first bishop of Elmham was Beaduwine or Badwin,[38] he attests a grant of land in a charter dated 693.[39] It was in this same year that the East Anglian King Anna's daughter Etheldreda founded the great abbey at Ely. Bishop Nothberht followed Badwin; his attestations appear on two charters, one of 706 concerning land in Worcestershire, and the other, land in Kent.[40] Bede writing in 731 says 'at the present day Aldberht and Heathulac were bishops in East Anglia'.[41] It was Heathulac or Hadulac who was in Elmham and Aldberht in Dommoc. Heathulac was followed by Aethelfrith in 736, and after him Eanfrith, and then to Ethelwulf, who is known to have attested a charter at the Synod of Brentford in 781 in which the bishop of Worcester surrendered the monastery of Bath to Offa king of the Mercians.[42] Bishop Alhheard followed; he is active from at least 785 to 805, as shown by his records of nineteen visits to various synods at Chelsea, Clofeshoh, and Alcaeh (two unknown sites). He also attended a legatine synod in 786, the first since the days of Augustine at the beginning of the 7th century, at which the power of Rome was re-emphasised, and the organisation of the church tightened. Alhheard would have listened to all of this, and no doubt would have conversed with King Offa, the man who had recently completed the great earthwork marking the western boundary of his kingdom, and the only European ruler, according to Stenton, to deal on equal terms with Charlemagne[43]. These meetings must have been grand affairs; on July 26th 805 at the synod, or witenagemot, of Alceah, twelve bishops with various other clerics met in the presence of the kings of Mercia and Kent.[44]

Sibba followed the much travelled Alhheard. Sibba attended three of these great meetings in the company of the King and Queen of Mercia, various bishops, abbots, and others. His last meeting was on the 27th July 816 at the Council of Chelsea. In the text of the account of this meeting is *'Honorabilesque orientalium Anglorum episcopi Sibbano et Tidfritho'*. Tidfrith was senior in his years as bishop of Domnoc and yet here takes second place to Sibba of Elmham. Does this mean that the see of Elmham had become more important than that of Domnoc by the early ninth century, or are the names just arranged in alphabetical order? There are two other pointers to the possible dominance of Elmham over Domnoc. The first is that early writers state that it was the bishop of Elmham who anointed Edmund king of the East Angles in 856, and the second, that the new bishopric in Norfolk was named Elmham rather than Domnoc. William of Malmesbury wrote that the two sees of Domnoc and Elmham became impoverished by the actions of the kings of Mercia and Wessex, and as a consequence the bishoprics were merged to form a single see of Elmham. (Well before the Danish defeat of Edmund in 869). There is some confusion on this issue concerning the timing of the end of the see of Domnoc, it has generally been assumed that both sees ended with the defeat of Edmund by the Danes.[45]

After Sibba came Hunferth, and for this bishop we have a written record of his profession to Archbishop Wlfred in around 816 to 824. Like most of these, the text concerns the devotion of the new bishop to God, and the diocese, and the reverence and affection he shows to his archbishop, but tells us nothing more about the man or about the diocese.[46] It is possible that he is the same man mentioned as accompanying bishop Alhheard to the synod at Clofeshoh in 803 when he was described as diaconus or deacon.[47]

In about 824 the last of the pre-Danish incursion bishops was appointed. His name was Hunberht, a man who played an important part in the history of South Elmham, and of the whole East Anglian Kingdom. The part he played will be discussed on page 103. Like those before him he attended several councils, three were at Clofeshoh, two at Kingston, and his last one in London on Sunday the 8th November 845.

In 960 AD Theodred bishop of London wrote his will which included the phrase 'at Hoxne at mi bishoperiche'.[48] This seems to indicate that he had taken on this extra task following the disastrous Danish destruction and death of Hunberht nearly 100 years earlier. In 955 AD the series of bishops of Elmham restarts with Eadwulf. It is unlikely that he was at South Elmham only 9 miles away from Theodred, indeed it would seem almost certain that he was at North Elmham. This arrangement of two bishops probably continued until 1066 when the Domesday Book describes Hoxne as the seat of a bishopric before 1066. If this is so, we do not know the names of the Hoxne bishops, unless they are among the unidentified bishops mentioned in the registers of synods.

By 1070 AD the last Saxon bishop of Elmham had been replaced by the first Norman who moved his see to Thetford, and so the name Elmham as a diocese lapsed, and East Anglia became a single see again, after over 400 years. It seems that, except for the four years of 1066-1070 and possibly a brief period in the mid ninth century, neither of the Elmhams had been the single see of East Anglia.

Summary.

The collected evidence above suggests that the second East Anglian see established in 673AD was initially at South Elmham, and that it persisted at that site, probably becoming the dominant see, until the disaster of the Danish invasions and the death of Edmund in 869 AD. Recovery from this assault was slow, but by the mid 10th century the bishop of London had established a see at Hoxne and a new bishop of Elmham was in place at North Elmham. The choice of North Elmham as a site for the see was perhaps influenced by the presence of a cluster of ecclesiastical estates in that region. Thus both Elmhams had been the seat of the bishop. South Elmham had held the see from 673 AD to 869 AD, 196 years, and North Elmham from 955 AD to 1070 AD, a period of 115 years. We will probably never know whether organised Christian activity continued at South, or North Elmham, or neither, in the 86 silent years between 869 and 955.

[1] Bede. *Ecclesiastical History of the English People*. Book I chapter 25 and others. Penguin Classics (1990)

[2] William of Malmesbury. *The Kings Before The Conquest*. Book I. Para. 48. Llanerch Enterprises (1989)

[3] Bede *Ecclesiastical History of the English People*. Book III Chapter 18

[4] Ibid. Book II Chapter 15

[5] Norman Scarfe. *The Suffolk Landscape*. Alastair Press. (1987) pp. 81-82

[6] Peter Warner. *The Origins of Suffolk*. Manchester University Press. (1996) p. 204

[7] Elizabeth Rees. Celtic Saints in Their Landscape. J.H.Haynes (2001) Page 7

[8] Jonas. Life of St.Columban http://www.fordham.edu/halsall/basis/columban.html)

[9] The Times. 4th December 2002

[10] Bede. *Ecclesiastical History of the English People*. Book III Chapter 19.

[11] Richard Morris. *Churches in the Landscape*. Giant Phoenix. (1997) p.119

[12] Bede. *Ecclesiastical History of the English People*. Book IV. Chapter 13.

[13] A.Suckling. *The History and Antiquities of The County of Suffolk,* (1846) Vol.I p.183

[14] Copinger. *The Manors of Suffolk*. (1905)

[15] V.B. Redstone 'South Elmham Deanery.' Proceedings of The Suffolk Institute of Archaeology and History. Vol. XIV. (1913) pp. 324-331

[16] W. Hudson. 'The Norwich Taxation of 1254'. Norfolk and Norwich Archaeological Society. Vol. XVII. (1910) pp. 46-157

[17] Richard Morris. *Churches in the Landscape*. Phoenix Giant Paperback. (1997) pp. 128-129

[18] John Blair *Bampton Anglo-Saxon Minster*. Current Archaeology. Vol.XIV. (Nov. 1998) No.4 p. 124

[19] John Ridgard 'References to South Elmham Minster in the Medieval Account Rolls of South Elmham Manor'. The Proceedings of The Suffolk Institute of Archaeology and History. Vol.XXXVI. (1987) pp. 196-199

[20] Peter Warner. *Origins of Suffolk*. Manchester University Press. (1996) p. 132

[21] Walter de Gray Birch. *Cartularium Saxonicum* Vol. III (1893) BCS 1008.

[22] Norman Scarfe. *The Suffolk Landscape*. Alastair Press. (1987) p.115

[23] Hills C. et al. 'The Anglo-Saxon cemetery at Spong Hill, North Elmham'. East Anglian Archaeology.Vol. 6 (1977), Vol. 11 (1981), and Vol. 21 (1984)

[24] Wade-Martins. 'The Anglo-Saxon Dioceses in East Anglia'. East Anglian Archaeology Report No. 9. (1980)

[25] For details of these see East Anglian Archaeology Vol. II (1980) p. 247

[26] Stephen Heywood. 'The Ruined Church at North Elmham'. Journal of the British Archaeological Association. Vol. CXXXV (1982) pp. 1-10

[27] Wade-Martins. 'Excavations at North Elmham, an Interim Report'. Norfolk Archaeology. Vol. 34. (1969) p. 336

[28] 'The First Register of the Norwich Cathedral Priory'. Norfolk Records Society. Vol. XI (1939) pp. 23-37

[29] J.J.Raven. *History of Suffolk*. (1895) p. 49

[30] Martin Carver. 'Kingship and Material Culture in 'Early Anglo-Saxon East Anglia'. Origins of the Anglo-Saxon Kingdoms. Ed. S. Bassett. Leicester University Press (1989) p. 155

[31] Suckling. *History and Antiquities of the County of Suffolk*. Vol. I. (1846) p. 209

[32] Gillingwater. Lowestoft Record Office. Reference no. ES 876/8

[33] Dorothy Whitelock. *The pre-Viking Age Church in East Anglia*. Anglo Saxon England I. Edited by Peter Clemoes at al. Cambridge University Press. (1972) pp.1-22.

[34] Frank Stenton. *Anglo Saxon England*. In The Oxford History of England. Clarenden Press. 3rd Edition (1971) p. 256

[35] Norman Scarfe. *The Suffolk Landscape*. Alastair Press. (1987) p.123

[36] Henry Harrod. 'On The Site of The Bishopric of Elmham'. Proceedings of The Suffolk Institute of Archaeology and History. Vol. IV. (1864) pp. 7-13

[37] Peter Wade-Martins. 'Excavations at North Elmham 1967-8 an Interim Report'. Norfolk Archaeology. Vol. 34. (1969) p. 366

[38] Bede. *Ecclesiastical History of the English People*. Book IV. Chapter 5

[39] Walter de Gray Birch. Cartularium Saxonicum. Vol. I. (1885) BCS 85

[40] Ibid. BCS 116, and 91.

[41] Bede. *The Ecclesiastical History of the English People*. Book V. Chapter 23

[42] Walter de Gray Birch. *Cartularium Saxonicum*. Vol. I. (1885) BCS 241

[43] Frank Stenton. *Anglo-Saxon England*. In The Oxford History of England. Oxford. (1971) p. 215

[44] Walter de Gray Birch. *Cartularium Saxonicum* Vol. I. (1885) BCS 322

[45] Dorothy Whitelock *The pre-Viking Age Church in East Anglia*. Anglo Saxon England I. Edited bt Peter Clemoes et al. Cambridge University press (1972) p.19

[46] Walter de Gray Birch. *Cartularium Saxonicum* Vol. I (1885) BCS 375

[47] Ibid. BCS 312

[48] Ibid. Will of Theodred, Bishop of London. Vol.III. BCS.1008

Chapter IV

Place Names

Elmham.

There are still a few names that reflect South Elmham's important Saxon past. The name Elmham itself is undoubtedly Saxon. The first written record being in a charter recording the Council of Clofeshoh held on Thursday 12th October 803 at which the bishop of Elmham signed himself as "Elmhamis Aecclesiae Episcopus".[1] Margaret Gelling considers that most of the Ham names in East Anglia were in use in Raedwald's time (593-617 AD).[2] In her "Place Names In The Landscape" she explains that Ham went out of use by about 650-700 AD, while Hamm continued to be used. The two terms have different meanings, Ham meaning village, hamlet, manor, estate or dwelling, while Hamm meant land hemmed in by water or marsh, a river meadow, or cultivated plot on the edge of woodland or moor. Ham certainly seems to fit South Elmham better than Hamm. Elm is a common prefix and is the Anglo-Saxon word for elm tree.

But is the origin of Elmham really as straightforward as this? Other interpretations have been made. Dr. Newton raises the possibility that it is linked to the personal name Helm.[3] In the Anglo-Saxon poem Beowulf, Queen Wealhtheow, is possibly described as "Helmes dohtor" or the daughter of a remote figure called Helm. In the "Widsith", a probable 7th century poem in the Exeter Book, (a collection of ancient poetry left to Exeter by the 11th century Bishop Leofric) the "Helmingas" was used as an alternative name for the "Wulfingas". The marriage of Wealhtheow to Hrothgar brought together two royal families, the Wulfingas or Wuffingas of the East Angles and the Skyldingas of the Danes. Where are the places with names including Helm or Helming? The most obvious is Helmingham, a village about 6 miles south of Debenham, and about 10 miles northwest of the ancient Royal Township of Rendlesham. There is a lost village in Norfolk also called Helmingham, which was in the present parish of Morton-on-the-Hill, a few miles northwest of Norwich overlooking the river Wensum from the south. North Elmham lies about 12 miles to the northwest of it. Elmham does not have the convincing aural similarity to Helmingas especially when compared with the spelling given in the earliest charter of 803 AD. But in this charter the attestations are in an 11th century copy of the original. A more reliable early source is the charter of the profession of Hunferd as bishop of Elmham (AD c. 820). Here three sources give the genitive form as Helmanensis, Helmaniensis, and Helmeanensis.[4] If, as is so often suggested, King Sigebert (a Wuffinga) gave the land at Elmham to his first bishop Felix, might his own ancient family name have been given to it, as Dr. Newton suggests? Finally it is worth pointing out, in this same context, that the Anglo-Saxon words for alms were Almes or Aelmes, and that Aelmeshand meant alms giving, or charitableness. Could the charitable gift of Sigebert to Felix have given us the name Elmham? This too seems a long shot.

Flixton.

Flixton first appears in the Domesday Book as Flixtuna in 1086. The name has been given the meaning "farmstead or village of a man called Flick".[5] Norman Scarfe agrees that Flick is a common Suffolk name, but cannot trace it back any further than 1542.[6] He further points out that the Bishop of East Anglia held both the Flixton in South Elmham and the Flixton in Lothingland in 1086, and that these lands may be a relic of King Sigebert's possible gift to Saint Felix himself. Margaret Gelling explains that the suffix 'tun' was not in common use before 750, it may therefore be likely that these villages were not named in this way until at least a 100 years after the death of Saint Felix.[7] If Norman Scarfe were right, why would Felix's name have been given to these villages? Were any of his sacred relics taken to them, and did they become places of pilgrimage? There is no evidence for this. William of Malmsbury says that Felix died at Domnoc, and that his body was translated to Seham. (Now identified as Soham in Cambridgeshire) The Liber Eliensis (the 12th century Book of Ely) also says that he was buried at Seham, and that a famous monastery was founded there. The same document quotes another source as saying that Felix himself founded a monastery at Seham and at Redham (Reedham) in Norfolk. The Chronicle of the Abbots of Ramsey Abbey describes the further translation of Saint Felix's remains from Soham to Ramsey. There is nothing here to suggest that relics went to either of the Flixtons, nor of the establishment of an early Flixton monastery. It seems most likely that the names record the veneration of the Saint, and his ownership of the land, land that remained in the hands of the church until well after the Norman Conquest.

Homersfield.

"Bishop Aelmer held Humbresfelda before 1066, one manor of five carucates of land. Now Bishop William holds (it)." So says the Domesday Book. The name Homersfield may be derived from the personal name Hunbeorht, and feld. As mentioned above, Norman Scarfe has very reasonably linked the name of Hunberht, who became Bishop of Elmham in 824, to this. In the five ninth century charters in which his name Hunberht appears it never has the letter O in it.[8] Nevertheless in The Dictionary of English Place Names (A.D.Mills 1991) the name Humbresfelda is said to have the meaning "open land of a man called Hunbeorht", and the temptation to equate Hunberht with Hunbeorht is strong.

Saint Cross.

The other seven parishes' saintly names are easier to understand though one of them has the two names of St. Cross, and St. George. Suckling attributes the name St. Cross to both the armorial cognisance of the saint, and to the sandy nature of the soil near to the church, thus also Sandcroft. St. Cross is not generally sandy, and the Saxon meaning of the word croft is small field. Nevertheless, Sandcroft was clearly the name of the place in 1319 when Robert de Sandcroft was patron of the church there. It has also been reasonably claimed that the village gave its name to Archbishop Sancroft, who had been reared in Fressingfield during the first half of the 17th century, and subsequently played a leading part in many of the great events of those turbulent times.

The word cross is of course a non sequitur when preceded by saint, but The Cross does have its day. Holy Cross day (14th September) has been celebrated in the East since AD 335. This recalls the day that St. Helena discovered the Holy Cross buried on Golgotha. She was the British mother of the Emperor Constantine. In the West, Holy Cross day is May the 3rd.[9] Helena was said to have been the daughter of a fabulous king Coil of Essex but Gibbon favours the tradition that she was an innkeeper's daughter.[10] If so she would have been associated, in some way, with the Roman system of post-houses and their 'mansii', set along the major highways to accommodate important travellers.[11] The Holy Cross is remembered at Holyrood in Edinburgh. Why should it not be remembered in Elmham by the corruption of the Latin Sanctus Crux to St. Cross?

There are 157 place names in England commemorating saints. Eighty-eight of these are to local saints and most of these are in Cornwall, leaving 69 in the rest of England, of which ten are in South Elmham and Ilketshall.

This is therefore a rare concentration of saintly parishes. **St. Peter's parish** was referred to in the early 14th century by the obviously Scandinavian name of Joltorph, or Yolthorp, raising the possibility that all the parishes were named at some later date, but other 14th century documents in the Lowestoft Record office clearly refer to the parishes of St. Margaret, All Saints, and Sandcroft.[12]

The ancient track called Uncles Lane running from the northern end of All Saints common to the northwest, and forming the boundary between All Saints and St. Michael's parishes, may have had its origin in the Anglo-Saxon word *uncuo* meaning strange or unfriendly, or in the Scandinavian personal name of Unkyll. The Old Norse word 'bekkr gives the name to South Elmham's stream, the Beck.[13] An Old English word 'hulver', originally 'hulfere', meaning holly, said to be a 'lost word' found only in place names, but still used occasionaly in Suffolk, lingers in the district as a farm name in St. Michael's parish.[14] Oliver Rackham writes that holly trees were pollarded, and their branches used as forage, in spite of their sharp spines.[15]

[1]   Walter de Gray Birch. *Cartularium Saxonicum*. Vol. I. (1885) BCS 312

[2]   Margaret Gelling. 'A Chronology for Suffolk Place Names'. The Age of Sutton Hoo. Editor Martin Carver. The Boydell Press. (1992) p. 56

[3]   Sam Newton. *The Origins of Beowulf and The Pre-Viking Kingdom of East Anglia* D.S.Brewer (1994) p. 134 Footnote 2

[4]   Walter de Gray Birch *Cartularium Saxoicum*. Vol. I. (1885) BCS 375

[5]   A.D.Mills *A Dictionary of English Place Names*. Oxford University Press (1991)

[6]   Norman Scarfe. *The Suffolk Landscape*. Alastair Press. (1987) p. 127

[7]   Margaret Gelling. 'A chronology for Suffolk Place Names'. The Age of Sutton Hoo. Ed. Martin Carver. Boydell Press. (1999) pp. 56-57

[8]   Walter de Gray Birch. *Cartularium Saxonicum*. Vols. I, and II. (1885-87) BCS 379, BCS 384, BCS 386, BCS 421, and BCS 448..

[9]   Vernon Staley. *The Liturgical Year*. A.R.Mowbray & Co. Ltd. London. (1907) pp. 101-105..

[10]   E. Gibbon. *History of the Decline and fall of The Roman Empire*. World Classics. Oxford University Press. Vol. I. (1906) p. 446

[11]   P.Salway. *Roman Britain*. The Oxford History of England. Oxford University Press. (1991) p. 568

Place Names

[12] Lowestoft Record Office
    1. Early 13th century land conveyance in **St. Margaret**
    (Cat. No. HA12/B2/ 3.7)
    2. November 1336 Land conveyance in **All Saints**
    (Cat. No. HA12/B2/2.48)
    3.1336 A grant by Robert de Sandcroft in South Elmham
    (Cat.No.HA12/B2/3.9)
    4. February 1340 Land conveyance in Homersfield
    (Cat. No.HA12/B2/3.4)
    5. 13th century South Elmham court roll refers to Sancroft Hall (ES 741/B2/)
[13] Margaret Gelling. *Place Names in The Landscape*. Phoenix Press. (1984) p. 14
[14] A.D. Mills. *A Dictionary of English Place Names*. Oxford University Press.
  (1991) p.??
[15] O. Rackham. *The History of the Countryside*. Phoenix Giant (1998) pp.120, and 141

Chapter V

The Old Minster

The enigma of this impressive ruin has aroused the interest, and stimulated the speculation of successive generations of historians, architects, and other interested people, as to its date and function. It lies on a sloping site, within a rectangular earthwork, just to the west of a stream in the parish of St. Cross. (See Plates XI and XII) There is no indication that what is left of the building is likely to give up any of its secrets to those of us who now have an interest in it. Nevertheless, it is worth collecting and reviewing the evidence that is available, in an attempt to illustrate some possible explanations for its existence. This is yet further speculation, but speculation based on a broad examination of the ever increasing literature on medieval history and architecture.

A Description of the Ruin.

The ruin is eccentrically placed within the earthen ramparts of what is probably a Roman fort, an area of about $4^1/2$ acres of sloping uncultivated land bordering a small tributary of the Beck. (See Figure II) Its walls are not oriented in line with the surrounding earthworks. Various attempts to reveal associated buildings either by geophysical detection using resistance, or magnetic measurements, or small excavations have failed to find anything of importance. Two trial trenches across the north and west ditches revealed a few small Roman pottery sherds. In a trench to the south of the ruin was a small curved gully, and in this was some late Roman pottery. Two small fragments of a middle Saxon pot were found to the south west of the ruin.

Most of what we know about the building comes from the study made by Smedley and Owles during the summers of 1963 and 1964.[1] The structure itself is divided into three spaces, a western narthex, a nave, and an apsidal eastern chancel. It has an internal measurement of about 90 by 27 feet, and, except for its eastern end, is rectangular. (See Figure III) At the eastern end, and projecting 20 feet at its maximum, are the foundations of a rounded or apsidal wall (now below ground level). Some parts of the main walls still stand 14 feet high. The walls are made of flint and mortar, and the surface flints are arranged in courses without any patterning. There

An Enigma of Ancient Suffolk

Figure II

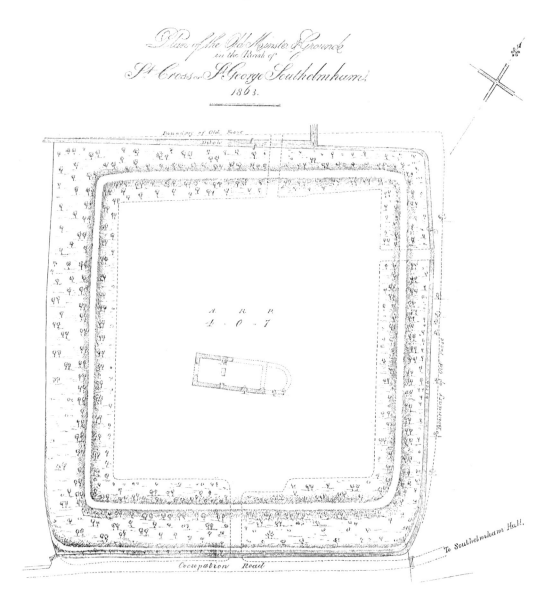

Plan of Old Minster Site

This plan dated 1863 is taken from a paper by B.B.Woodward
'The Old Minster South Elmham' in The Proceedings of The Suffolk
Institute of Archaelogy Volume IV 1864.

By permission of The Suffolk Institute of Archaeology and History

The Old Minster

Figure III

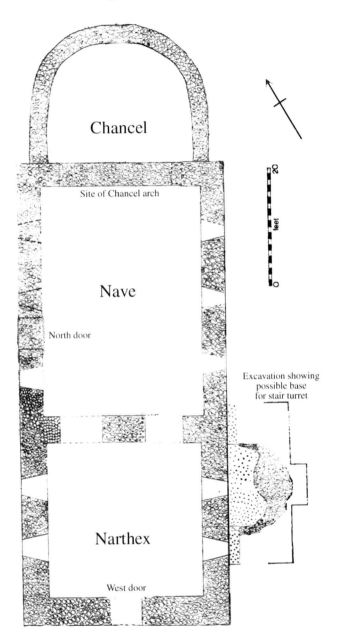

Chancel

Site of Chancel arch

Nave

North door

Excavation showing
possible base
for stair turret

Narthex

West door

Ground plan of the Old Minster South Elmham
as shown by the 1963 excavations.

Taken from The Proceedings of The Suffolk Institute of Archaelogy Vol XXXII. Part I. 1970

By permission of The Suffolk Institute of Archaeology and History is some evidence of layer coursing; an effect produced by building in horizontal layers of about one foot in height to allow the mortar to harden, but this is seen only on the inside of the wall between the two north windows of the narthex. (See Plate IX) The walls are not all the same thickness, those forming the narthex are the thickest at 4 feet 7 inches, those of the nave 4 feet, and those of the apse only 3 feet.

Within the structure there are two other features. The first is the massive cross wall of the narthex 26 feet from the inside of the western end; this wall has two 7-foot openings symmetrically placed at either end. On the south side, it is claimed that the springing of the arch can be seen at 10 feet 8 inches above the original floor level, though this is not something that I can see. The second feature is not visible above ground level but was

Plate XIV

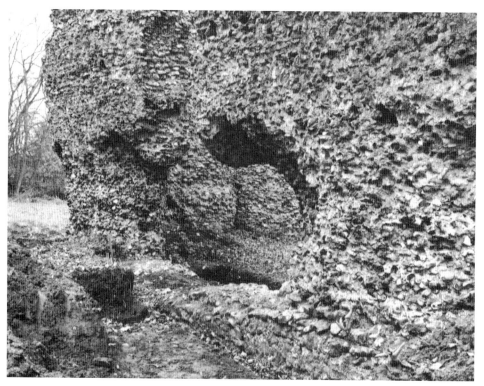

A photograph of the western end of the Old Minster taken in 1963 by P.H. Harrold.

It shows that the worn step mentioned by Smedley and Owles, is not ashlar but cobbles revealed during the 1963-4 excavations. It is a foundation lying across the junction between the apse and the rest of the building, its ends are not bonded into the sidewalls, they butt against them suggesting that it was a later addition. There seems no means of knowing the form of the chancel arch at South Elmham. The springing of the arch on the south side is said to be visible (though not to me) at only 7 feet above the ground. The absence of any remnant of the apse walls above ground level, and the evidence that the foundation, which abuts between the bases of the arch is a later addition, suggests to me that this foundation may have been the base of a wall filling in the arch after removal of the apse.

The southerly sidewall has five single splayed window openings set with their sills about 7 feet above the ground. In the northerly wall only three remain, but in that wall excavation revealed a five foot door opening set at about 27 feet from the beginning of the apse, and displacing the window to the west of it by about two feet to the west, compared with the window in the south wall. The evidence for this doorway is now below the ground. At the western end of the building is a centrally placed opening, now very much widened in its lower part by removal of the flint work, but originally five feet wide. At the base of this, and beneath the present ground level, is 'a very worn step' set 1 foot 3 inches above the original floor level.[2] (See Plate XIV) This photograph, taken by P.H.Harrold at the time of the excavations of 1963-4, suggests the step was not made from a single slab of stone, as suggested by the description 'very worn', but was cobbled. Looking higher up the opening the real width of the doorway can be seen, and the remnant of an arch starting at 10 feet 3 inches above the step on the north side. (See Plate XV)

The building has only three pieces of freestone left in it, but evidence that the rest has been removed is perhaps seen best on the internal openings of the windows in the north wall, where there are jagged interruptions to the line of flint work. (See Plate XVI) These windows, and those on the south wall also, have an internal splay of about four feet narrowing to two feet externally. One of the windows in the south wall is almost complete to its summit, where the arch seems to have been rounded rather than pointed. (See Plate XVII) At the time of the 1963 excavations on The Old Minster, two pieces of worked stone were found below ground at the southeast corner of the nave forming quoin, or corner, stones. The top piece (see Plate XVIII) was removed and is now in the possession of the owner of the minster Mr. John Sanderson. The lower piece remains buried. One other substantial dressed stone was found buried outside the southwest corner of the narthex. Although evidence for previous dressed stonework is easily seen on the internal surfaces of the building, evidence for external stonework is far less convincing, both as quoins, and as window dressing. (See Plate XIX)

Outside the narthex adjacent to 15 feet of the south wall and projecting 11 feet outwards, was an area of rubble and cement. The margins of this area were not well defined, and there was no suggestion of any deep foundations like those for the walls.

Where has all the rest of the ashlar stonework gone? If any has been used for domestic buildings perhaps it is seen at the south east corner of South Elmham Hall. It is not evident in any other local houses, though there are three large slabs of ashlar forming the threshold of an ancient barn, the foundations of which are still visible on the adjacent site of Greshaw Green. The rest might well have been used in the parish churches of South Elmham, where much of the stonework has evidence of being recut for new positions. (See the west window in St. Peter's, the chancel door arch in St. Michael's, (Plate XXXI) and many other places.)

Another feature of the walls is the presence of many putlock holes. The wooden putlock was the horizontal member of the scaffolding used in construction. The failure to fill these at The Old Minster has been used as evidence that it was never finished. But there are many examples of unfilled putlock holes in completed churches still standing, perhaps the best, and most relevant, is the Saxon tower of Sompting church in East Sussex. (See Plate XXVII) These would probably have been filled with plaster internally, and a rendering externally, which has subsequently decayed.

One of the most unique features of The Old Minster is that it seems to stand, in its remnant, as it was originally built without obvious evidence of any alterations, except possibly the demolition of the apse, and the walling in of the chancel arch.

Discussion of the architecture and dating.

What chances are there of dating this unique and ancient structure? 'Anglo-Saxon Architecture' by Taylor and Taylor is a most comprehensive and learned study of the subject. These authors, writing in 1965, concluded that *'the Old Minster was begun at a period when the Danes were active, or becoming active in East Anglia; that it was placed for defence within the existing moat and rampart, which were either made for the purpose or was already existing; and that in spite of the precautions, the building of the church was stopped by the Danish invasion'*. [3] (The first recorded Danish raids in East Anglia were in 841.[4]) '*The early Anglo-Saxon characteristics and the unfinished and unoccupied state of the church would both fit this hypothesis, which would place the church in the period A3 or B.*' (of Baldwin Brown, that is, 800 to 850 AD.) It was the single splay windows, the tall narrow west door built without recessing, the apsidal end, the possible triple chancel arch, and the excellence of the mortar, that they thought indicated an early Anglo-Saxon date.

Nikolaus Pevsner in 1974 describes the plan as curious giving it a tripartite interior like Bradwell and Reculver in the 7th century. The church he says is mysterious in purpose, in date, and in plan.[5]

On October 4th 1897 J.T.Micklethwaite (surveyor to the dean and chapter of Westminster Abbey) examined foundations beneath the site of the chancel arch hoping to find evidence of the bases of two columns that would have formed a triple chancel arch. He did not find them, but he noticed that the sides of the arch would have been 21ft. apart, and that a single arch to span this would have been so high that its proportions would have been different from any found elsewhere in early work. He considered that the substantial continuous foundation beneath the arch would not have been put there unless it had something to support.[6] At the Saxon church of All Saints Brixworth (Northamptonshire), there was a triple arch between the nave and chancel, and here the columns had separate foundations. The 7th century church at Reculver (Kent) also had a triple chancel arch, and the two columns from it are still preserved in the crypt of Canterbury Cathedral. The suggestion that there may have been a triple chancel arch is interesting, and if true would certainly give the building an early date of construction, but the evidence for it is not very strong. However we interpret this part of the building, the foundation beneath the opening of the chancel arch looks like an alteration because it abuts but is not continuous with the rest of the foundations, and therefore is evidence against the building being unfinished, as suggested by Taylor and Taylor.

Stephen Heywood writes that the quoin stones found in situ at South Elmham were typically Norman in size and in their diagonal tooling.[7] Smedley and Owles' report mentions only three quoin stones one of which was a fragment of Saxon grave slab the other of similar size lay beneath it, (the third lay beneath the north west corner of the narthex). They did not describe this second piece in detail but the photograph in their paper does give the impression that there may have been diagonal tooling, and the reworked fragment of grave slab certainly shows diagonal tooling. (See Plate XVIII) Heywood also considered that the single splay windows with ashlar dressings, and the walls of neatly coursed flint facings with rubble and mortar core were post Conquest. The 'typically Norman' neatly coursed flint work is certainly there, interspersed in places with some larger flints and erratic stones on the outside of the south wall, a feature that Hart describes as Anglo-Saxon, but warns us that the distinction between this and Norman work is very much blurred.[8] One of the oldest round towers in East Anglia is at East Lexham (Norfolk), perhaps dating from the 9th century, and here the flint work is neatly coursed in horizontal layers. (See Plate XX) On the inside of the north wall of the narthex between the windows there is a segment of wall showing what Hart calls 'layer coursing', a feature which is of no help in dating. This appearance is of horizontal bands of about one foot high representing what could be safely made before leaving to allow the mortar to harden. Unlike bricks the flints are non-absorbent and tend to move under pressure in wet mortar. (See Plate XIII)

Return now to the two pieces of worked stone found to be forming a quoin, or corner, of masonry at the southeast corner of the nave interior. The top piece was considered to be crucial evidence for the date of construction of the building because it was decorated with interlace work on one surface. It was likened to the decoration on a Saxon tomb slab at Milton Bryan, Bedfordshire. The Elmham fragment is undoubtedly very like this Bedfordshire stone (see Plate XXI) which is scathingly described by T.D.Kendrick as rude, rustic, and naively monotonous, exploiting only the most universal of the English barbaric designs, namely the interlace panel. Kendrick dates the stone as early 11th century, but gives little evidence to support this.[9] The difficulty of dating carved Saxon stonework is well reviewed by David M.Wilson.[10] Smedley and Owles thought that the fragment found at The Old Minster could not be earlier than the 9th century, and as there were signs of weathering before being broken and used as a quoin stone, they suggest that the building of the Minster was in the 10th or more likely 11th century. They considered the possibility that it might have been used as a repair, but concluded that it was bonded in such a way as to preclude this. Their photograph of the stones does not help us to understand why they came to this conclusion, and the position of the stone, adjacent to the chancel arch base, raises the possibility that it may have been put in place at the time the foundation across the chancel arch floor was constructed, and therefore may not be part of the original fabric.

If, as suggested above, the apse at South Elmham Minster was demolished, it is reasonable to ask why? Might it have been because of a structural fault in the unusually large chancel arch, or possibly just because of changes in architectural fashion? Whatever the reason, the excavations in 1963-4 show that all the furnishings of the apse had been removed. What might they have been? Two mysterious and ancient pieces of worked stone lying beneath the bishop's throne in Norwich Cathedral may be ancient relics of the early Saxon sees of East Anglia. C.A.Ralegh Radford made a detailed analysis of these two fragments of stone in 1961.[11] He concluded that the northerly fragment was part of a throne, and that the shape of the back of the stone suggested that it had originally been placed against the semicircular seating commonly found around the inside of the apsidal wall (called a synthronon). On the northern face of the stone was the much damaged appearance of an interlace pattern, consistent with an 8th century date, and certainly pre-Conquest. The southerly fragment of stone was much smaller and may have come from the synthronon itself. Both fragments had been damaged by intense heat, and by weathering. Radford thinks that it is very unlikely this damage was caused by the fire in the cathedral in 1171, or that the weathering occurred in Norwich. He suggests that these stones were relics of the old bishopric of Elmham, and later Thetford, and that they had been moved to Norwich from there. However, if the stones had been cut before the Viking raids of the 9th century, it follows that they had probably been made for the see at Domnoc, or South Elmham, and then removed to North Elmham when the bishopric was re-established in the mid 10th century. It is possible therefore that these ancient stones were in the ruins of the apse of The Old Minster at South Elmham, where they would have been weathering for nearly a century. There has never been any suggestion that there had been a fire at The Old Minster, and so the burning of the stones may have occurred later, at some other site. Perhaps the most likely site was North Elmham where Sweyn Forkbeard could have burnt them on his dreadful progress through Norwich to Thetford in 1004 AD. The stones were obviously highly venerated at the time they were installed in the new Norwich Cathedral; perhaps this veneration arose from a tradition that they had been parts of the throne used by the last pre-Viking bishop of Elmham, who may have been the only bishop in East Anglia at that time.

What now of the mass of rubble and mortar lying to the south of the narthex wall? In what seems to me a misguided enthusiasm to liken The Old Minster to the ruin at North Elmham, Smedley and Owles suggest this is the base of a stair turret like the one at North Elmham, though it is very much larger than the turret, and does not seem to have an adequate foundation for a turret, nor are there any signs of an entry through what remains of the narthex wall. The stair at North Elmham has its entry at ground level, from inside the building; there is certainly no evidence whatsoever for this in the south wall of the narthex at South Elmham. It is much more likely that this was the place where the builders of the minster prepared and mixed mortar. It is obvious that large amounts of mortar must have been used to build the walls. This would have been mixed on site, usually in a hollow in the ground, adjacent to, or as at Stow Church in Lincolnshire actually inside the north transept.[12] Unfortunately the description of the rubble and mortar platform makes no mention of its depth, and the plan drawn in their figure 6 shows that the excavation went no deeper than two feet at the most. The raft like foundations of the minster walls were fully five feet deep, nothing like this lay in the rubble and mortar platform. The misconception that there was a turret stair to a chamber above the narthex, like that at North Elmham, was important because it influenced Smedley and Owles into thinking the building was late.

Comparisons with other early church buildings.

A short manual by A.H.Thompson called 'The Ground Plan of the English Church' makes no mention of The Old Minster but assembles the evidence for the ground plans of early Saxon churches.[13] These plans are based on the Roman basilicas, initially secular buildings used for commerce and as halls of justice. They were aisled halls with apsidal ends, members of the judiciary would sit around the apse, and oaths would be taken on a centrally placed altar. This plan was adapted for use by the early Christians and in the 4th century they were building great churches in Rome, and some like the 6th century Sant Apollinare Nuovo in Ravenna, retain their original structure, with its western entry through a vestibule or narthex, its aisled nave, eastern apse, and altar. (See Figure IV).

In England, the first Saxon churches to survive to the present day in any form, came with St. Augustine's mission in 597 AD. Of these, eight still remain, seven in Kent and one in Essex. Most are ruins, but two of these are still in use, St. Martin's in Canterbury, and St. Peter's On The Wall at Bradwell in Essex. All were built on or very near to Roman sites. St. Martin's is built from reused Roman materials, and is in part, the remnant of an earlier Roman church. St. Peter's Bradwell is on the wall of a 'Fort of The Saxon Shore' called Othona, and is made from reused Roman building materials. These Roman forts of the Saxon Shore, eleven in all, were built in the 3rd century for reasons that are still uncertain, certainly defensive,

Plate VIII

Stone Street looking north over Ilketshall St. Lawrence

This shows the junction between the absolutely straight southern section
and the northern part of the road that follows the ancient field pattern.

Plate IX

Stone Street looking south over Ilketshall St. Lawrence

Plate X

Two Saxon Cremation Jars found near Beccles

They are between 6 and 7 inches tall and may be like those said to have
been found at The Old Minster.

By kind permission of the Curator of Beccles Museum

Plate XI

The site of The Old Minster

Marked by the rectangular group of trees in the centre.

Plate XII

The Old Minster ruin seen from the south west. March 2003.

Plate XIII

The internal face of the north wall
of The Old Minster showing layer coursing.

Plate XV

The last remaining evidence of the arch
of the western entry to The Old Minster.

Plate XVI

Evidence for stone robbing at the internal angle of a
window in the north wall of The Old Minster.

Figure IV

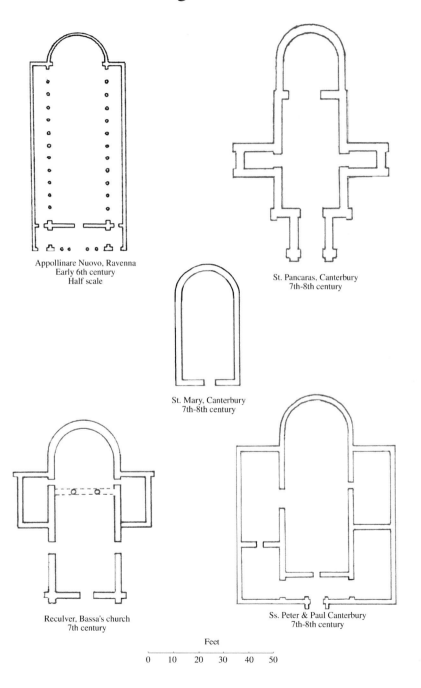

Appollinare Nuovo, Ravenna
Early 6th century
Half scale

St. Mary, Canterbury
7th-8th century

St. Pancaras, Canterbury
7th-8th century

Reculver, Bassa's church
7th century

Ss. Peter & Paul Canterbury
7th-8th century

Feet

0   10   20   30   40   50

Early church ground plans

but also possibly as trading stations.[14] Reculver church was within the walls of another Fort Of The Saxon Shore called Regulbium on the north Kent coast (see Figure IV). The church at Lyminge (Kent) was built on the site of a Roman domestic building. At Rochester (Kent) the church was within the Roman city walls. Three other ancient church foundations are at the site of St Augustine's abbey itself, just outside the walls of the Roman town of Durovernum (Canterbury), they are St. Peter and St. Paul's, St. Mary's, and St. Pancras. (See Figure IV) There was another small Saxon church (the foundations of which are lost beneath a Norman rebuild) within the Saxon Shore Fort of Richborough (Kent).

These very early churches had entries at their western ends either through a small porch, as with St. Pancras (Canterbury) or directly into the church as at St. Mary's (Canterbury) or as in St. Peter and St. Paul in Canterbury, where there was an internal wall forming a vestibule or narthex. They had an apsidal eastern end, and some had side chapels entered from within the nave. At Bradwell, and at Reculver, two columns producing a triple arch supported the chancel opening. None of them had western towers.

This simple plan has been used at The Old Minster South Elmham, where there may also have been an early Kentish influence. Bertgils Boniface was bishop of Domnoc from 652 to 670 AD and Bede tells us that he was a Kent man. Norman Scarfe has pointed to Boniface as the most likely builder of The Old Minster[15], (though in the new edition of his book 'The Suffolk Landscape' 2003 he describes him as 'just possibly'). This would put its date of construction very much earlier than any other estimate, and three years before the establishment of the new diocese of Elmham.

St. Nicholas' Church, South Boarhunt in Hampshire is a late Saxon building, and, though it is much smaller, it has the same feel as The Old Minster, with a nave, a chancel, and a western entry, and I think gives us a clue as to its external appearance. (See Plate XXIII) Also, internally, there had been a wall across the nave about 13 feet from the west end, forming a narthex. It had a narrow chancel arch of 6 feet 6 inches with blind arches either side giving a three arched appearance to the east end of the nave. (Not an original feature) The total internal length of the church is about 40 feet, and the width of the nave 19 feet. The chancel is rectangular. There is now a gallery at the west end lit by a window of uncertain date in the west wall. Windows to the north and south are later additions; there is no evidence of other openings to light a first floor room. This little church seems to have had a narthex, and has no tower.

The Old Minster

There are many other churches with similar ground plans that are much later. St. John the Baptist church in Finchingfield Essex is a 12th century Norman structure with a surprisingly similar plan. It has an elaborately decorated doorway at the western end, and a thick walled, originally two storey, entrance, almost as wide as the nave. This structure by this time was called a 'westwork' and may be a relic of an early German influence of the later Saxon period. There is no evidence for an apse, which by then was going out of fashion. Another Norman church of similar design is St. Mary at Brook in Kent. Here the westwork, with its first floor as a priest's chamber with an altar in its eastern wall, has been developed into a massive tower, again the same width as the nave. There is a rectangular chancel narrower than the nave. (See Plate XXII) These churches are both smaller than The Old Minster, which at 90 feet by 27 feet is an enormous building when compared with any of its local parish churches. All Saints church, one of the largest, is 48 feet long and 15 feet wide internally, and is still only 26 feet 7 inches wide when the aisle is included.

Heywood[7] argues that the churches at North Elmham, South Elmham, and Brook in Kent, are all Norman and have similar status as the personal chapels of the bishops at their country residences. His main point is that they all have similar western ends. Heywood's drawing of a reconstructed North Elmham church gives it a western tower, and we know that St. Mary at Brook (Kent) has a massive western tower, both of these have an internal measurement of 21 feet. But can there be any conviction that The Old Minster had a tower? The sheer size of the narthex 26 feet square internally makes this unlikely. The impressive Norman tower at Finchingfield Essex is only 19 feet in its maximum internal measurement, and the great central towers of the Norman cathedrals at St. Albans in Hertfordshire, and Norwich, have internal dimensions of barely 30 feet. On the other hand why did they make the narthex wall 7 inches thicker than the nave wall? Was the cross wall that forms the narthex a structural necessity to support a tower, avoiding the need for a wide archway, or was it just needed to make a three chambered building? These questions may forever remain unanswerable, but it does seem likely that the slightly thicker narthex wall did support a first floor chamber, thus making this part of the building taller than the nave. Access to this would have been by an internal wooden stair, for there is no evidence for an external entry, nor is there any evidence in the remaining internal masonry for a stone stair.

Hardy and Martin have likened The Old Minster to the cell of the Norwich Cathedral Priory at Hoxne built by Herbert De Losinga in 1100,

Figure V

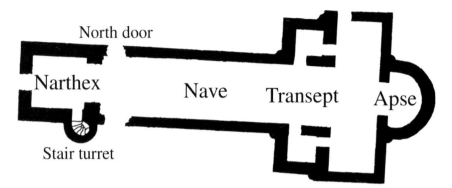

The ruined church at North Elmham

Taken from 'The site of the Anglo-Saxon Cathedral and Bishop's North Elmham'
Published by North Elmham Parish Council 1998 and compiled by Stephen Heywood

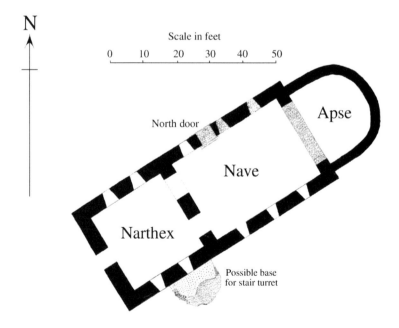

The Old Minster South Elmham

Taken from 'Smedley and Owles paper in Proceedings of the Suffolk Institute of
Archaeology Vol XXXII part I 1970

North and south Elmham ruins to the same scale
showing their orientation

of which nothing now remains. They suggest that The Old Minster was a similar cell, and that it was abandoned when a new chapel with cloisters was built on the manorial site.[16] The account rolls of South Elmham Manor suggest, by the absence of any reference to the minster in the names of the ways and lanes of the estate, that The Old Minster had fallen into disuse by the mid 14th century.[17]

The ruined church at North Elmham Norfolk was built on the site of three previous wooden structures that may have been the cathedral buildings of the pre-conquest East Anglian see. There was no evidence that the wooden structures predated the Danish invasions, but in the adjacent North Elmham Park extensive and meticulous excavation has revealed a sequence of 45 buildings dating from the 7th to the 12th centuries.[18] One group of buildings has been interpreted as the halls and out buildings of the 10th century bishop's palace. In the upstanding ruin at North Elmham there is good evidence for a 'westwork' with an external stair to the first floor and a west doorway at ground level. This westwork was the same width as the nave, and together they formed a long rather narrow interior 92 feet by 21 feet, ending in a transept and beyond this an apse, giving a total internal length of 121 feet. (See Figure V) Heywood has challenged the opinion of Rigold that the ruin has Saxon origins[19]. He has done this mainly on the evidence of the few remaining pieces of stonework, but also the quadrant pilasters, (rounded columns of flintwork at the junction of the nave and transept walls). These he says are reminiscent of Norman round tower work and the radiating chapels at Norwich Cathedral.[20&21] Heywood's reconstruction of the ruined church at North Elmham shows that it was a more complex building than The Old Minster. (See Figures VI, and VII) If Heywood is right, what we see in the ruin at North Elmham is the Norman work of Bishop Herbert de Losinga subsequently altered by Bishop Despenser to form his fortified manor house. Herbert having revamped this building, also founded the adjacent new parish church of St. Mary, as Bartholomew Cotton tells us.[22] Heywood raises an interesting comparison between the similar transept flanking towers at North Elmham and those at St. Trond Abbey in Lotharingia. Lotharingia, in the Low Countries, may have been the place of origin of Herbert's family and given them the family name of Losinga. Herbert later moved to Fecamp in Normandy where he became prior.[23]

Do these comparisons help us to date The Old Minster? Unfortunately not very much, the great variety of design both before and after the Conquest really makes this question unanswerable. Although there are

Figure VI

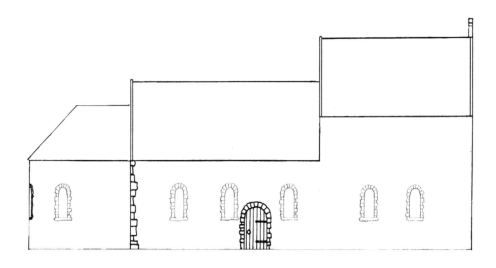

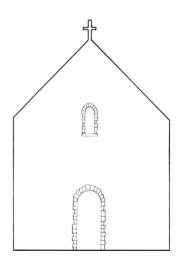

The north and west elevations of the possible
appearance of the Old Minster South Elmham

some churches that are obviously Saxon, like St. Mary's Brixworth (Northants), and some that are obviously Norman like Norwich Cathedral, there is in many a confusion of style reflecting the lack of a smooth universal progress in design and construction, after the radical change from timber to stone.

Could The Old Minster have been the cathedral of the diocese of Elmham?

If The Old Minster is an early Saxon building, it is big, in fact larger than the earliest stone minster at Winchester, and probably therefore important. The single splay windows have been taken as an indication that the building is Norman, but Taylor and Taylor explain that the typical Saxon double splay windows were a late development. They gave some advantages in ease of construction, and in the weatherproofing, that a mid wall opening had, as opposed to an outer edge opening.[24] For this reason there is a case for thinking that if the structure is not Norman it is of early Saxon workmanship, and certainly older than the Viking incursions of the mid 9th century. The form of The Old Minster is more in keeping with the early Kentish churches, but the relationship between form and function is poorly understood, and therefore form cannot be used as an indicator of cathedral status. The site, a Roman fort that may well have had evidence of pagan activity as a Saxon burial ground, was typical for early Saxon Christian settlement. The choice of such sites was in accordance with Pope Gregory's advice, in his letter to Abbot Mellitus in 601, in which he recommended that pagan temples should not be destroyed but converted to Christian use.[25]

To our eyes it is also very isolated, and so far, there is no evidence that it was ever otherwise. This isolation favours a monastic function. But the paucity of evidence of Saxon sites near to The Old Minster may just reflect the absence of meticulous archaeological investigation, or the systematic ploughing out of all the evidence, or erosion of the sloping site, or a combination of these things.

Was access to the site as difficult as it now seems to be? The road from Homersfield to South Elmham Hall after a dog leg bend in the Beck valley at St. Cross, veers east as it crosses the stream that comes down from The Old Minster site, but before this change in direction it is running in line with the stream and the footpath a little further up beside it, looking very like the wavy lines of the coaxial field system further east. This track would have linked it to the important route up and down the Waveney valley. Some support for this track comes from Alfred Toms vicar of Flixton who wrote in 1915 (concerning Flixton Priory): *'In 1264 an important addition was made to the revenues of the Priory by the grant of the rights of a water mill. The site of this water mill, together with some remains of an ancient road probably leading from the bishop's palace of South Elmham, is associated with a fordable place in the river Waveney, still occasionally used by huntsmen.'*[26] The Reverend Toms gives no source for this statement, nor does he suggest which mill is referred to. The most obvious fordable place would be beside Homersfield bridge, which is not far from the old Homersfield water mill. There are no other crossings indicated on the first Ordnance Survey map of 1837. A network of four footpaths leading to the Minster is shown on the 1905 6 inch Ordnance Survey map, these, if they are ancient, together with the major route up and down the Waveney valley, might favour its use as a secular rather than a monastic building.

If the most important local route of communication was the Waveney valley, it is reasonable to ask whether the river was ever navigable beyond Bungay? This would surely depend on the size of vessel. Suckling quoting Abbo of Fleury, who was at Ramsey Abbey in the late 10th century, writes that Eye at that time was in the midst of a marsh, and that the rivulet thence to the Waveney had been navigable. He also writes that at the time of Kett's rebellion (1549) a small pinnace was prepared to take 20 men up the Waveney to Weybread. [27] It is very likely therefore that the river was navigable both up and down stream from Homersfield.

The Old Minster may have had quite good routes of communication with the Waveney valley settlements both in Norfolk and Suffolk, and could have been a good site for the second East Anglian see; but there remains the most crucial issue of dating the ruin, and this rests almost entirely on guesswork. Nevertheless, however unlikely, the possibility remains that it was the cathedral building of the early diocese of Elmham.

If it was not the cathedral, where was the cathedral?

It may be more likely that the cathedral was a wooden structure on a site referred to in the 14th century Manor of South Elmham Rolls as 'Eldhallestede' a field name for high ground near to South Elmham Hall.[17] (See Map I) In the south east of England most of the very earliest churches would have been built of timber, except for those where Roman cut stone and bricks were available, as mentioned above. Field walking on the possible site of 'Eldhallestede' in St. Margaret, near to South Elmham Hall, has revealed 7th century pottery and a fragment of Mid Saxon window glass. Subsequently more pieces of Saxon glass have been found on the site. (Personal communication M.J.Hardy) Fragments of glass such as these have been found on ecclesiastical sites, particularly in Northumbria and at Glastonbury, but also at Thetford, and are strong evidence for the presence of an ancient church. These finds are in the pocket-like extension of the south west part of St. Margaret's parish that includes a quarter of the moated South Elmham hall site, strongly suggesting its ancient importance.[17] (See Map I) A geophysical survey in 2001 (Friars to Flyers Project II, Suffolk 2001/95) showed short ditch-type anomalies that may represent occupation remains, but no clear pattern to suggest substantial settlement features. This part of St. Margaret has never been subjected to any more intense archaeological investigation. Here the meagre evidence is a tantalising invitation to further archaeological research.

If The Old Minster was not the cathedral what might it have been?

In form The Old Minster can be likened to both the earliest Saxon churches of the 7th and 8th centuries with their western entries, eastern apses, single splay windows, and the absence of a tower, and on the other hand to the similar late 11th and early 12th century structures like St, Mary's at Brook in Kent, and St. John the Baptist at Finchingfield in Essex. St. Mary's at Brook is of special interest because the first Norman Archbishop, Lanfranc, apportioned it to Christchurch Monastery at Canterbury in 1076. The question arises therefore as to whether the first Norman bishop of Norwich, Herbert de Losinga, built The Old Minster as a cell of his priory in Norwich, rather than as his personal chapel as suggested by Heywood above, perhaps knowing that it was near the site of the earlier see of the East Angles. The 13th century document called 'The First Register of the Norwich Cathedral Priory' may be of some help here.[22] (Bishop Herbert.) *'This man of prudent council not content with the harm arising from his wandering seat being at one time in a wooden chapel in the village which is called Elmham, and at another time indeed at the little town of Thetford, in a church of another persons estate, or in any other places whatsoever at the whim of the different bishops, he at great cost secured himself the site at Norwich…'*

This is the written evidence that the see was at a wooden church in the village of Elmham. But which Elmham is the document referring to? Nowhere is South Elmham referred to as a village. Copinger says that it is variously referred to as a 'liberty', a 'manor', or a township in 'ancient times.'[28] This, the reference to Thetford, and the physical evidence for a wooden church found beneath the ruin at North Elmham,[29] makes it probable that The First Register was referring to the village of North Elmham.

A later entry in The First Register was as follows:

(Bishop Herbert) *'Then the bishop, wishing to procure the patronage of many holy places for himself, built quite anew the church at Norwich in his court, another at Elmham and a third at Lynn, all of which he gave to the monks of Norwich and made them over completely to their control'.* Which Elmham was this and which church did he build there quite anew? There seems little doubt that this was the parish church of St. Mary North Elmham, though little now remains of the original structure. The only remaining Norman feature that I found was a small window opening high on the south wall of the chancel. The Cotton documents give us no written evidence that Herbert built anything at South Elmham.

Deirdre Wollaston writes that among all the letters of Herbert de Losinga there is no mention of architecture, but there is evidence of his impatience with his monks that throws light on the activity engendered by church building.[30] It is in his 14th letter as follows: *'But alas the work drags on, and in providing materials you show no enthusiasm. Behold, the servants of the King and my own are really in earnest, gather stones, carry them to the spot when gathered, and fill with them the fields and ways, the houses and courts; and you meanwhile are asleep with folded hands, numbed as it were, and frostbitten with a winter of negligence, shuffling and failing in your duty through a paltry love of ease.'*

Further entries in The Register do concern South Elmham. (Bishop Herbert) *'In Suffolk, I have given also Elmham which I bought of William Neveris; …'* and later: *'Further, I give to them (the monks serving God in our cathedral church) the whole tithe of Cressingham Hall and the third part of the tithe of the demesne Hall of Sechford and of Elmham, and of Humeresfelde, and all these things I concede to be free of quit from all service, custom and exaction forever which have been granted for the benefit of the monks in all their uses.'*

Ridgard considers that this purchase recovered the site of The Old Minster for the bishopric, and that this satisfied Herbert's desire to own places sacred to the history of the diocese.[17] The demesne Hall of Elmham may represent the buildings that stood on the present site of South Elmham Hall, but may refer to the older hall remembered in the field name 'Eldhallestede' mentioned above. The site of demesne Hall of Humeresfelde (Homersfield) is unknown, though it is likely to have been associated with the site of the church.

On the whole these fragments of evidence do not give any support to the concept that The Old Minster was a Norman structure built by Herbert de Losinga. Further than this the orientation of The Old Minster is very different from any of the churches that we know Herbert had built. The Old Minster is aligned 30° north of due east, (see Figure V) whereas the churches that he built are all oriented to within 12° of due east; at Norwich (the Cathedral 11.5°), King's Lynn (St. Margaret's 9°), North Elmham (St. Mary's 12°), North Elmham ruined bishop's chapel (4°) and Great Yarmouth (St. Nicholas 9.5°). Only 4% of the 642 churches studied by Cave deviated more than 30° from east.[31] It is perhaps more likely that it was an earlier monastic foundation. This would be in keeping with the isolation of the building, the substantial central cross wall shielding the monks from being seen by the laity, a feature considered important as early as the 7th century when Jonas tells us that Columbanus, the Irish monk at his monastery in Luxeuil, was not prepared to allow laymen to enter the dwelling of the servant of God. But that he had prepared an alternative and suitable place where all who came would be received.[32] A monastic use for The Old Minster would not preclude it from a function as an old minster, in the late Saxon sense of being the centre of a deanery, serving the whole of South Elmham.

Summary.

How can such a confusion of information be summarised? Not easily, but these are my thoughts. The first East Anglian bishopric was set up in 630 AD at a place called Dommoc or Domnoc. By about 673 a second bishopric was established at Elmham. This was initially at what we now call South Elmham, and the site of the cathedral was either The Old Minster or in a field anciently named 'Eldhallestede' on high ground near to the present South Elmham Hall moated site. After the destruction caused by the 9th century Danish raids, Christian organisation was disrupted. It gradually returned in the mid 10th century, at first through the efforts of the bishop of London and his East-Anglian see at Hoxne, but also by the appointment of a new bishop of Elmham based at North Elmham. Thereafter the bishopric at Hoxne lapsed, and the bishopric at North Elmham moved, first to Thetford, and then to Norwich.

Perhaps none of this has much to do with The Old Minster, the date of which is so difficult to assess. Most opinion is against it being the original Elmham cathedral, but it is unreasonable to discount this completely. The Old Minster certainly has a 7th century design. It also may have been built

Figure VII

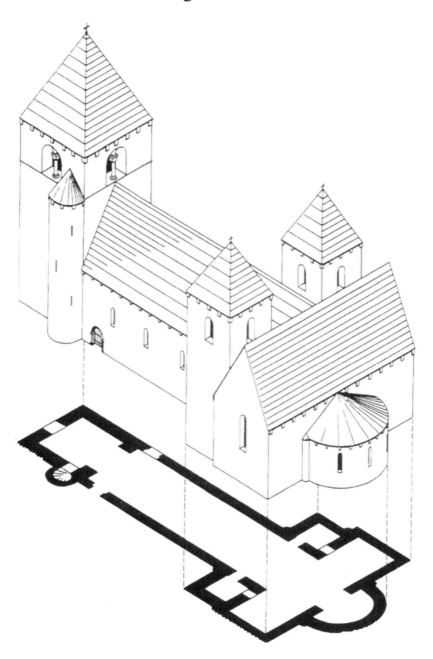

Stephen Heywood's isometric reconstruction of the ruined church at North Elmham

By kind permission of Stephen Heywood

in the early 10th century, after recovery from the Danish incursions, or much less likely two centuries later in the early post Conquest era. The notion that it may have been built in 906, the year of the translation of the body of St. Edmund to the new abbey at Bury St. Edmund, will be discussed in the Chapter VII on Orientation of The Old Minster. The external appearance of the building would have been plain and undecorated, quite unlike Stephen Heywood's reconstructed, elaborate, North Elmham building. Figure VI illustrates my own concept of the external appearance of The Old Minster, and Figure VII Stephen Heywood's carefully reconstructed appearance of the North Elmham building.

It is strange that although small ancient artefacts like pottery, metalwork, bone tools, wood, and other plant and animal materials can be dated with some certainty, science has so neglected dating of ancient buildings. It seems to me that there may be a way out of this paradox by the analysis of mortar. Mortar is formed from a mixture of slaked lime (calcium hydroxide) sand, and water. It hardens as the atmospheric carbon dioxide reacts with the lime to form calcium carbonate (chalk). In this way mortar behaves like plants and should be amenable to radio active carbon dating techniques. So far no process has been developed to do this, but if such a method were found it would revolutionise our ability to date buildings like The Old Minster. Until then we can continue guessing.

[1] N. Smedley, & E. Owles. 'Excavations At The Old Minster, South Elmham'. Proceedings of the Suffolk Institute of Archaeology and History. Vol. XXXII (1970) Part I. pp. 1-16

[2] Ibid. p. 11.

[3] Taylor and Taylor. *Anglo-Saxon Architecture*. Cambridge University Press. (1965) pp. 231-3

[4] The Anglo-Saxon Chronicles Winchester manuscript A. 838 (841)

[5] N. Pevsner. *Buildings of England*. Second Edition. Suffolk. Penguin (1974). p. 427

[6] J.T. Micklethwaite. 'The Old Minster at South Elmham'. Proceedings of the Suffolk Institute of Archaeology and History Vol. XVI. (1918) pp. 30-35

[7] Stephen Heywood. 'The Ruined Church at North Elmham'. Journal of the British Archaeological Association. Vol. CXXXV. (1982) pp. 1-10

[8] Stephen Hart. *Flint Architecture of East Anglia*. Giles de la Mare. (2000) p. 20

[9] T.D. Kendrick. *Late Saxon and Viking Art*. Methuen. (1949) p. 82

[10] David Wilson. *Anglo-Saxon Art*. Thames and Hudson. (1984) pp. 53-56

[11] C.A.Ralegh Radford. 'The Bishop's Throne in Norwich Cathedral'. Archaeological Journal. Vol. CXVI. (1961) pp. 115-135

[12] Warwick Rodwell. *The Archaeology of The English Church*. Batsford. (1981) p. 115

[13] A.H. Thompson *The Ground Plan of the English Church*. Cambridge University Press. 1913.

[14] Andrew Pearson. *The Roman Shore Forts*. Tempus. 2002. pp.156-163

[15] Norman Scarfe. *The Suffolk Landscape*. Alastair Press. (1987) p.119

[16] M.J.Hardy, and E.A.Martin. 'Field Walking in South Elmham' Proceedings of the Suffolk Institute of History and Archaeology. Vol. XXXVI. (1986) pp. 233-4

[17] J. Ridgard. 'References to South Elmham Minster in the Medieval Account rolls of South Elmham Manor'. Proceedings of the Suffolk Institute of History and Archaeology. Vol. XXXVI (1986) pp. 196-200

[18] Peter Wade-Martins. Norfolk Archaeology. Vol. 34. (1969) p. 366

[19] S.E. Rigold. Medieval Archaeology. Vol. VI-VII. (1962-3) pp. 67-72

[20] Stephen Heywood. 'The Ruined Church at North Elmham'. The Journal of British Archaeological Association. Vol. CXXXV (1982) pp. 1-10

[21] Stephen Heywood. 'The Romanesque Building' *Norwich Cathedral; Church, City, and Diocese 1096-1996*. Hambleden Press. (1996) p. 89

[22] The First Register of Norwich Cathedral Priory. Norwich Records Society. Vol. XI. (1939) pp. 23-37

[23] Deidre Wollaston. 'Herbert de Losinga' *Norwich Cathedral, Church, City and Diocese 1096-1996*. Hambleden Press. Page 22-23. 1996

[24] Taylor and Taylor. *Anglo Saxon Architecture*. Cambridge University Press. (1965) pp. 836-837

[25] Bede. *Ecclesiastical History of The English People* Book I Chapter 30

[26] Rev. Alfred Toms. *Records of Flixton*. Richard Clay. (1915) p. 8

[27] Rev. A. Suckling *The History and Antiquities of The County of Suffolk* London (1846) pp. vi & vii

[28] Copinger. *The Manors of Suffolk*. Vol. 7, (1905) p. 170

[29] Wade-Martins. Norfolk Archaeology. Vol. XXXV. (1972) pp. 416-428 & 25-78

[30] Deidre Wollaston. 'Herbert de Losinga' *Norwich Cathedral, Church, City, and Diocese. 1096-1996*. Hambleden Press. (1996) p. 32

[31] C.J.P. Cave. 'The orientation of Churches' Antiquaries Journal Vol. 130 (1950) p. 48

[32] Jonas' Life of St.Columbanus. Paragraph 33 at http://www.fordham.edu/halsall/basis/columban.html

Chapter VI

Other Ancient Buildings in South Elmham

Of the churches in the 'saints' Flixton is one of the earliest. By the mid 19th century the old tower was leaning and the 13th century chancel derelict. It was rebuilt in stages during the Victorian era. The architect Anthony Salvin designed the new tower in 1856 as an accurate copy of the original.[1] There is a description of the original church by Suckling in 1846, who thought that it was Saxon.[2] It runs as follows:

'The church at Flixton comprises a square tower, a nave with a north aisle, and a ruined chancel. The tower is, by far, the most ancient portion of the edifice, being unquestionably of Anglo-Saxon construction. It is built entirely of uncut flints, laid in rude horizontal courses, and is at present entered from the body of the church, through an arch, enlarged in its eastern wall about the time of Henry III, if we may judge by the fashion of the pillars which sustain it. The original entrance was beneath a low triangular-headed arch on the western side; which has been recently discovered by the removal of a coat of plaster from its interior face. On each side of the lower part of the tower is a circular aperture, equally splayed inside and out. A stage higher, we have on the west, a circular-headed window, splayed at the sill, but not at the jambs or arch. In the next stage, on each side is a circular-headed window, deeply splayed within, so as to leave but a small narrow aperture on the external face of the wall. The jambs of these windows are very far from the vertical, inclining towards the arch, and being wider at the bottom. On each side of the belfry is a balustre window. The balustre is a cylinder of equal thickness throughout, and is surmounted by the ordinary Norman cushion capital. (see Plate XXIV) The arches and the jambs of the windows are made up of rag and flint, and here and there a large smooth pebble. The outside face of the arch, with part of the soffit adjoining, is coated with rough-cast. The tower leans fearfully to the south-west, in consequence of the subsidence of its foundations. At what period this took place is unrecorded, but it evidently occurred subsequently to the thirteenth century, as the pillars of the arch in its western wall, constructed about that period, are thrust out of the perpendicular by the

declination of the tower. The ascent to the bell stage is by means of a very steep and rude ladder, of curious construction. The north aisle is divided from the body of the church by four pointed arches sustained by pillars, each of which is composed of four clustered columns, in the style prevalent in our third Henry's reign. We may conclude, therefore, that the old Saxon church, attached to the tower was demolished about that era, and the present fabric constructed on its site.'

Suckling goes on to tell us that within the church beneath the communion table was the ancient altar stone made of black marble and marked by the five crosses representing the five wounds of Christ. This he thinks must have been removed from the ruined chancel before the reformation. Here then was a rare relic of prereformation church furniture.

Plate XXIV

Cushion capital in the original window of the Saxon tower of Flixton church
Taken from Suckling's History of Suffolk 1846

Plate XVII

The south west window of The Old Minster,
which shows the most complete window arch.

Plate XVIII

The grave slab fragment from The Old Minster
showing the interlace pattern and the reworked face
with its diagonal chisel marks.

The slab fragment is 1 foot 5 inches long.

Plate XIX

The north west corner of The Old Minster showing
little evidence for freestone robbery.

Plate XX

East Lexham Church Saxon tower
showing horizontal coursing

Plate XXI

Saxon Grave Slab from Milton Bryan Bedfordshire
Compare with plate XVIII

Plate XXII

The western entries to St. Mary's at Brook in Kent
(left), and to St. John The Baptist Finchingfield, Essex.

Plate XXIII

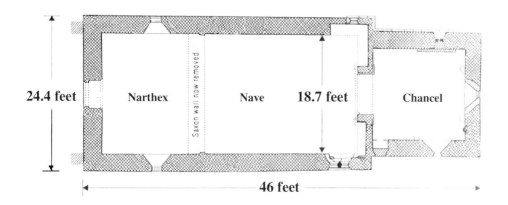

Saint Nicholas Boarhunt, Hants, with its ground plan.

Plate XXV

A watercolour painting of Flixton Church
in the 1840's before it was rebuilt in 1856.
Painted by G.L.Simes for the architect Anthony Salvin in preparation for
his work on the church. (RIBA drawings collection)

It was at the council held at Winchester in 1076 that Lanfranc, the first Norman archbishop of Canterbury, decreed that all altars should be made of stone, and it was later decreed that they should be marked with five crosses. Nearly five hundred years later Edward VI and again Elizabeth I ordered their removal. There are at least two other black marble altar stones that have been rediscovered and reinstated, one at St. Mary's Brook (Kent) the other at St. Clement Old Romney (Kent). The one at Flixton still awaits discovery. There is a more local example of a stone altar at Hales in Norfolk, where the Churches Conservation Trust under the guidance of Michael Gooch restored the altar by removing it from the floor of the chancel and putting it on a brick plinth. This altar stone is rough-hewn from blue lias, and bears the remnants of the five crosses on its upper face.

One earlier account of the church at Flixton comes from Gillingwater who saw it on 28th July 1796. This was as follows: ' *This building consists of two aisles separated by three pillars forming four arches. The chancel is totally in ruins, the bare walls containing the window spaces, only now remaining. ...... The steeple is square from top to bottom; its materials are stones and mortar, except a small part near the top of it, which is formed of bricks, and appears more modern than the lower part, and was added, probably, to repair some damage the tower had received from storms. This structure appears to be extremely old, and is inclined from the perpendicular towards the south, as is very evident from the arch forming the entrance thereto from the south aisle of the church, which is warped considerably. This steeple is extremely plain, being totally destitute of every kind of ornament, and has, thro' age, the appearance of an unseemly mass of stones and mortar uncouthly heaped on each other to a considerable height, and hastening to a ruinous decay. It contains three bells, and stands at the west end of the south aisle*'[3] This description seems to be at odds with Salvin's careful reconstruction of the steeple, which Pevsner describes as a Neo-Norman steeple familiar in the Rhineland. It is likely that the evidence that Salvin found lay within the tower, and this is supported by Suckling's description of a triangular headed arch hidden behind plaster in the tower, and by a small watercolour at the foot of the plan of Flixton church, which shows the tower and the chancel as Gillingwater describes it. G.L. Simes drew this plan prior to the work of Salvin.[4] (See plate XXV)

Looking now at the reconstructed building, many reused fragments of ashlar can be seen in the exterior of the tower wall. Several of these are cylindrical, and may be portions of the balusters mentioned by Suckling, and represent the only recognisable remnants of the earlier church. (See Plate XXVI) The best reminder of what the original Saxon church would have looked like must surely be Sompting church in East Sussex. (See Plate XXVII) These are the only two church spires in England of this 'typically Rhineland'design.[5] The beauty of the lines of Sompting tower, however, exceeds any of those in the Rhineland that I have seen.

Whatever the age of the building the site is likely to be much older. It is in a commanding position overlooking the Waveney valley, on a platform with its rounded northwestern edge steeply banked towards the valley floor.

Another very ancient site, at which Iron Age sherds have been found, is that of All Saints church. The aerial photograph (plate XXVIII) shows so well the ancient lines of the old field patterns (described in Chapter I). It also shows the line of an ancient track, still marked as a footpath on modern maps. It runs from the St. Nicholas road near Crabtree Corner through All Saints Church Farm yard, then between the moat and the graveyard, and on past The Elms ending near Blooms Hall on the boundary with Rumburgh. The only obvious remnant of this track now is in Church Farm farmyard itself, and that grassy patch between the moat and the graveyard. (See Map VI, and Plate XXVIII)

All Saints church is associated with this isolated farmhouse, with the old approach to the church through the farmyard itself. Richard Morris has used this complex as an example in his book 'Churches In The Landscape'.[6] Here he describes the frequent juxtaposition of church and lordly manor in the English landscape, and how sometimes the house is a grand mansion, and at others an isolated farmhouse. This illustrates the secular origin of our ancient parish churches as the products of local lords of the manor. In South Elmham all of the churches are mentioned in the Domesday Book, and were therefore present before the Conquest. More than this, the number of manors and churches in the Domesday Book for Elmham and Homersfield are the same. This gives strong support to the secular origin of these local churches. There is, however, no agreement on the dates of their construction. Pevsner finds no evidence of Saxon work in any of them. That enthusiastic amateur W.J.Goode takes a different view, and is in no doubt that the church at All Saints has Saxon features.[7] (Plates XXIX and XXX) He lists eight: the thin tower wall, the low original tower, fillets between tower and wall, upper doorway without dressed stone within the tower, tower arch with 3 inch set back head, six windows in the tower without dressed stone, a ledge to thin the tower wall at 18 feet 9 inches above ground, and a ledge to thin the nave west wall. His arguments for Saxon

Other Ancient Buildings in South Elmham

Plate XXVIII

All Saints church, and Church Farm on 16th June 1952.

See Capps Lane to the right and the similar line of the old track
running between the church and the farm, both in line with
the ancient field boundaries.

University of Cambridge Department of Aerial Potography.

workmanship in the nave and the tower up to the stringcourse are compelling. He brings a sweet logic in his introductory chapters on round tower church architecture that is difficult to gainsay. Proof, however, remains elusive, but might lie in the development of a method for carbon dating mortar (see page 83).

The other parish churches have no pre-Conquest features that are visible. Some of the reworked dressed stone may have come from The Old Minster, but there is no way of knowing this. St. Michael's parish church shows how reworked stone was used to form the doorway in the south wall of the chancel. (Plate XXXI) Some of the church walls could have pre-Conquest origins, but subsequently lost any identifying features, and others might have been made of timber alone, and left no remnant of their existence. The south east corner of St. Margaret's church has erratic stone instead of dressed stone as quoins, this could indicate a Saxon origin. The Norman doorways in the south walls of St. Margaret's, St. Peter's, and St. Michael's parish churches could be inserts in Saxon walls, but there is as yet no proof of this. (Plate XXXII) Some of the church sites have a much earlier feel about them, particularly Homersfield and Flixton churches, which stand high on rounded headlands overlooking the Waveney valley to the southwest. St. Margaret's church site, though not as striking, also stands on a rounded headland overlooking the Beck to the north. St. Peter's church stands on a rectangular site on high ground on the edge of the valley of the Beck, requiring embankment of its southeastern corner.

There are probably no other pre-Conquest buildings, or ruins, still standing in South Elmham, but the possibility remains that some of the village church walls are Saxon.

[1] Nikolaus Pevsner. *The Buildings of England. Suffolk*. Penguin Books. Second Edition. (1974) p. 214
[2] Alfred Suckling. *The History and Antiquities of the County Of Suffolk*. Volume 1 (1846) p. 202
[3] Gillingwater MS. Lowestoft Record Office. Ref. 89/7/9
[4] Royal Institute of British Architects Drawings collection Vol. 5. (1976) p. 62
[5] Nikolaus Pevsner. *The Buildings of England. Suffolk*. Penguin Books. Second Edition. (1974) p. 29
[6] R. Morris. *Churches in the Landscape*. Phoenix Giant. (1989) p.249
[7] W. Goode. *Round Tower Churches Of South East England*. The Round Tower Churches Society. (1994) p. 169

Chapter VII

Has the orientation of The Old Minster any hidden meaning?

The orientation of The Old Minster is not truly east west, but nearer to being northeast southwest. The compass bearing of the line of the south wall looking east is 62.5°. There is a correction of 2.75° to subtract from this for true north, giving a line of 59.75°. This is 30.25° away from being truly east, which would be 90°. This alignment is unlike the other parish churches in South Elmham, which are all facing east to within less than 10°, except for St. Peter's, which is 76°. (14° away from being due east), and is very different from the ruin at North Elmham. (See Figure V) There should have been no difficulty in aligning church buildings; a careful record of the shadow of a stake in the ground on any sunny day would have shown where due south was. Why did they get this wrong, and did they care, or was the misalignment intentional and does it give us a clue as to when it was built, who built it, and what its dedication was?

A drive for conformity and ecclesiastical discipline came with King Edgar and his Archbishop Dunstan in the second half of the 10th century. One of Dunstan's known concerns was for church orientation, and when visiting the new Mayfield church in Sussex he is said to have nudged it with his shoulder to put it in line![1] It has been suggested that both North Elmham and the South Elmham ruins are the chapels of the first Norman bishop of East Anglia, Herbert de Losinga. Neither of the Elmham ruins has a dedication. Unlike The Old Minster, the ruin at North Elmham is quite well orientated to within 4 degrees of due east. Is this an important difference? Morris in his brief discussion of church orientation rather suggests that it is, for when the cathedrals of Exeter, Wells and probably York were rebuilt they were also reoriented to the east, and he adds that there were signs that similar changes were made at village level. This is another important indication that The Old Minster was not built by Herbert.

Very little is written on the subject of church orientation. The Roman architect Marcus Vitruvius Pollio in De Archetectura (27 BC), advised that all temples should be oriented east west. The Emperor Charlemagne took this advice when building his great palace chapel at Aachen completed in

An Enigma of Ancient Suffolk

805 and still standing today[2]. Saint Benedict had nothing to say about church orientation in his famous 6th century Rules, and the various Nicean councils and their canons were silent on the matter. It is strange that the first written reference to church orientation, as opposed to temples, comes in Wordsworth's poem 'To The Lady Flemming' written in 1823.

> When in the antique age of bow and spear
> And feudal rapine clothed with iron mail,
> Came ministers of peace, intent to rear
> The mother church in yon sequestered vale;
>
> Then, to her patron saint a previous rite
> Resounded with deep swell and solemn close,
> Through unremitting vigils of the night,
> Till from his couch the wished for sun uprose.
>
> He rose, and straight – as by divine command,
> They who, had waited for that sign to trace
> Their work's foundation, gave with careful hand,
> To the high altar its determined place;

The poem has the following footnote: *'Our churches, invariably perhaps, stand east and west, but why is by few persons exactly known; nor, that the degree of deviation from due east, often noticeable in the ancient ones, was determined, in each particular case, by the point in the horizon, at which the sun rose upon the day of the saint to whom the church was dedicated.'*

In 1950 C.J.P. Cave wrote of his measurement of the orientation of 642 churches.[3] In this study he recorded the compass bearing looking east down the centre of the church's interior. His most interesting findings were that only 1.6% were pointing due east, and that there was a preponderance of 63.1% of churches oriented north of east, compared with 35.3% to the south. Around this slightly skewed axis of orientation, the churches orientations had a normal distribution. (That is that their orientations were evenly distributed either side of the axis) He concluded that this normal distribution proved that there was no connection whatsoever between the orientation of the churches and the bearing of sunrise on the feast day of the saint to whom the church was dedicated. On the other hand Hugh Benson has studied the orientation of churches in Oxfordshire in 1956 and found that about a third pointed in the direction of sunrise on their patronal days.[4]

The others may well have been rededicated, a common occurrence he says following the reformation. Cave had underestimated the complexity of estimating the position of sunrise at a church a thousand years ago. Benson emphasised the importance of measuring the angle of the horizon above or sometimes below the horizontal, the need to allow for refraction of light and to use the upper limb of the sun as the marker of sunrise. Of course there are then the calculations concerning the change from the Julian to the Gregorian calendar.

On the 4th of April 2002 I woke to find the early morning sky clear and sparkling with stars. I was up and standing within the ruins of The Old Minster before dawn eagerly awaiting the rising sun. It was a calm and silent morning and it seemed the sun would not appear, when suddenly the whole pale red disc was there sitting on the horizon. I took a compass bearing of it and recorded the time, and was left wondering how often it would be possible to see the sun as it rose, what chance would there be of seeing sunrise on a particular day in the year, and how many years one might wait before being able to do so. Using these findings I was able to check that at least part of the method for calculating sunrise described in appendix A was accurate.

Using the method described in appendix A, and The Old Minster's line of orientation of 59.75°, the elevation of the horizon at 0.845° and the date of 900 AD, the spring sunrise would have been in line with the orientation of The Old Minister on May 8th. The date of sunrise, for any line of orientation, regresses by one day for every added hundred years, thus for 1000 the sunrise would have been on May 7th. (See appendix B) This day did not coincide with any Saint's day that seemed relevant to The Old Minster. Realising the difficulties of knowing the position of sunrise both for the ancient church builders, and for us now to look back so far, there is a temptation to stretch the point and look either side of the date for a more likely dedication.

List of Saints Days near to May 8th.

23rd April St George
25th April St Mark
29th April St Edmund's Translation
1st May Sts. Philip and James
3rd May Invention of the Cross
6th May St. John The Evangelist
19th May St. Dunstan Archbishop Canterbury 960-88
26th May St. Augustine Archbishop Canterbury 597-604

The dedication date nearest to the calculated date with any local relevance is May 3rd, The Holy Cross day. This would be unusual as a church dedication, but could conceivably have influenced the naming of the parish. (For a discussion of the name St. Cross see page 49) But the 29th of April is a far more interesting, though slightly further removed, near coincidence, and is worthy of some more detailed discussion here.

April 29th 906 AD commemorates the translation of St. Edmund's uncorrupted body to the Abbey at Bedricesworth, later to be named Bury St. Edmunds. At this time the cult of Saint Edmund was very strong, both in England, and on the continent. This, now long forgotten day in the liturgical calendar, is surely an attractive option, and if we accept this as the builder's intention, it would mean that there had been an error of only 4° in the original orientation.

King Edmund died on the 20th November 869 AD (Anglo-Saxon Chronicle). The place of his death is not known, but Abbo of Fleury in his Passio Sancti Eadmundi written between 985 and 987 AD named it as Haegelisdun. This name can be equated only with Hellesden near Norwich that has no tradition as the site of martyrdom, or with some lost site.[5] Hermann, a Bury writer at the end of the 11th century, in his Liber de Miraculis Sancti Eadmundi 5 refers to Suthtuna (Sutton) as the first place of Edmund's burial, and that this was near to his place of martyrdom. Trefor Jones suggests that Edmund, after being defeated, might well have returned to the Wuffinga regal base at Rendlesham.[6] Here about 7 miles south is a place called Sutton (Suthtuna in 1086) and about 4 miles north is Hacheston (Hacestuna in 1086). This latter name he claims is like Abbo's Haegilsduna, though I have not found any discussion of this by place name experts, and Whitelock did not mention it. He goes on to say that the church at Bromeswell two miles south of Rendlesham has an ancient dedication to St. Edmund, and he says, the tradition that Edmund was tied to an oak tree when he was tortured could be remembered in the name of the village of Eyke, the old Scandinavian name for the oak tree. Another possible site for the martyrdom is south east of Bury St. Edmunds at Bradfield St. Clare, where there is a field named Hellesden, and two miles north a King's Hall, and a mile south Sutton Hall.

Yet, for all this, why has tradition placed the death of Edmund at Hoxne? That Hoxne was important in the 10th century is undoubted. In the mid 10th century Theodred, the bishop of London who revived Christianity in East Anglia after the Danish invasions, refers in his will to a church dedicated to St. Ethelbert at Hoxne, and that Hoxne was the site of his see in East Anglia, ('at Hoxne at mi biscoperiche'), but he makes no mention of Edmund in connection with Hoxne.[7] One and a half centuries later the foundation charter for Bishop Herbert de Losinga's Norwich Priory of 1101AD, gives us another point of view.[8] This charter grants to the Priory the church at Hoxne, *with the chapel of St.Edmund of the same village, were the same martyr was slain.*

Rivalry between Herbert de Losinga and the enormously wealthy abbey at Bury may well have prompted Herbert to claim that the site of Edmund's martyrdom was in his diocese at Hoxne. It seems likely that, at that time, as now, nobody knew where Edmund had died, and Herbert would have had freedom to invent the idea, to his advantage.

What relevance has all this to Elmham? An early 11th century document, The Annals of St. Neots, is the first extant reference to the accession of King Edmund in 855AD. It states that a year passed before he was crowned, and this was done by Hunberht the bishop of Elmham. Symeon of Durham in the early 12th century wrote that Hunberht was the unnamed bishop present at Edmund's martyrdom and that he shared this fate. Hunberht was the last bishop of Elmham before the Danish insurgence, and was consecrated in 824; he was the man who may have given his name to Homersfield (Hunbeortsfeld 1086 AD). If he were martyred with Edmund he would have been in his 70's, and would perhaps have been more likely, realising Edmund's hopeless situation, to advise him to surrender or to flee, which is what Abbo tells us he did. Abbo was a most learned monk, from Fleury on the Loire, who came to England and enlightened Ramsey abbey with his teaching. He was also an experienced hagiographer, and hagiography was the literary art of promoting saints, not of writing history. Nevertheless, if Edmund had followed Hunberht's advice and had run from the battlefield after his defeat, Abbo's account might seem to have been critical of him. Perhaps the only certain information about the death of Edmund is that in the Anglo-Saxon Chronicles for the year 869: 'and in that year St. Edmund the king fought against them, and the Danish took the victory, and killed the king and conquered all the land and did for all the monasteries to which they came.' (Peterborough Manuscript E)

This possible close connection between the martyrdom of Edmund, and Hunberht Bishop of Elmham, gave good reason to celebrate the translation of Edmund's body to the abbey at Bury by founding the building of The Old Minster in perhaps the same year, variously stated as between 900 and 906, and orienting it to face sunrise on the 29th April, the day assigned to this event.

An Enigma of Ancient Suffolk

The strange orientation of The Old Minster has therefore pushed me into a tortuous argument that suggests a building date of about AD 900. However unlikely, the argument seemed worth pursuing and stating here, if only to raise the important status of Bishop Hunberht in the affairs of East Anglia. Saxon bishops came and went without event, but here was one that South Elmham should remember.

[1] Richard Morris. *Churches in the landscape*. Phoenix Giant Paperback. (1989) pp. 208-9

[2] Paul Devereux. *Ancient and Sacred Places*. Brockhampton Press. (1998) p. 93

[3] C.J.P.Cave. 'The Orientation of Churches'. The Antiquaries Journal. Vol. 30. (1950) pp. 47-51

[4] Hugh Benson. 'Church orientation and Patronal Festivals'. Antiquaries Journal. Vol. 36. (1956) pp. 205-213

[5] D. Whitelock. Proceedings of the Suffolk Institute of Archaeology and History. Vol.XXXI. (1969) pp. 220 & 223

[6] Trefor Jones. *The English Saints*. Canterbury Press. Norwich. (1999) pp. 153

[7] Walter de Gray Birch. *Cartularium Saxonicum*. Vol.III. (1893) BCS 1008

[8] 'The First Register of Norwich Cathedral Priory'. Norwich Records Society Vol. XI (1939) folio 4d.

Chapter VIII

The Domesday Book Record of South Elmham

The two volumes of this record were produced in 1086 AD for William the Conqueror. The second unabridged volume, concerning Essex, Suffolk, and Norfolk is known as the Little Domesday Book. The first abridged volume concerned the rest of the country, and was named the Great Domesday Book. Fortunately for us the Little Domesday Book was in greater detail than the Great Domesday Book and is available to us now for the county of Suffolk in two volumes.[1] The English translation of 1783 by Abraham Farley, a translation that has never been bettered, is set beside the original Latin text. This gives the opportunity to study the ancient place names in their various recorded forms, and from the many scholarly footnotes, an understanding of the meaning of much of the text. There remain however many unexplained, and perhaps inexplicable, parts of the text. Who was W. the Constable in Ilketshall, and where, for example, were 'Croscroft' and 'Hetheburgafella' in the hundred of Wangford, and where was 'Rodenhala' in Lothing? These places that cannot now be identified, are as puzzling as other places that have ancient names and are omitted. At first sight the books seem full of promise for anyone trying to reveal some of the early history of South Elmham. In some respects this is true, but in many others the meaning remains arcane. Attempts to identify the present sites of the holdings described are thwarted by the vagaries of the entries. Measurement of land dimensions and areas are not easily amenable to interpretation. Much of what must have made sense to the locals in their manor, hundred, and shire courts is now obscure to us. A present day farmer in South Elmham would find the greatest difficulty in knowing who owned his land in the 11th century and how it was farmed.

The Little Domesday Book lists the ferding of Elmham as being in three parts, Flixtuna, Humbresfelda, and Almaha, (Elmeha, Halmeha) in the hundred of Wanneforda (Waineforda, Wenefort). The seven parish names of the 'Saints' are not mentioned, neither are the four parishes of Ilketshall, but as H.C.Darby points out, the population of both Elmham and Ilketshall in 1086 was large enough to suggest more than one settlement, and the record of several churches in these places tends to confirm this view.[2] (See tables I-XII for a summary of the 1066 Domesday Records for South Elmham and other local parishes) Failure to name the parishes does not necessarily mean that they did not exist, but just that their inclusion was unnecessary. Neither must we assume that they had the same names as they do now. A 14th century document refers to what we now call St. Peter's as Joltorph, or Yolthorp, and it may be that other parishes had such Scandinavian names before being named after their church's dedication.

Further difficulties arise with the recording of land areas. These are not assessed in real units but in hypothetical units of assessment for the King's gelds, or taxes. There is therefore a large discrepancy between the assessed acreage and the real acreage. The greatest discrepancy is in Elmham (see below). What was all this unassessed land used for?

	Domesday acres	Actual acres (Suckling)
Homersfield	776	981
Flixton	651$\frac{1}{2}$	1,761
Elmham	965	6,206 (Total of the 7 Saints)
Total	2,392 $\frac{1}{2}$	8,948

An attempt to summarise the entries for Elmham, Flixton, and Homersfield has been made in tables I-VI. This is a difficult and in places misleading summary, and nothing can replace examination of the texts themselves, but it does bring together the scattered information in a form that is more immediate for the reader. Look at the number of ploughs, 32 for Elmham, 20 for Homersfield, and 25 for Flixton in 1066, in all 77. Oliver Rackham used the number of ploughs in the whole of England in 1086 to calculate the area of grassland that must have been available at that time. Each plough, he said, required a team of eight oxen, and each animal required five acres of pasture[3]. For the whole of South Elmham this would give a total of 616 animals (8 x 77). This would have been increased to about 1,000 when the associated cows and calves were included. At about 5 acres per beast these would have required 5,000 acres of grassland. (There are only 8,948 acres now in the whole ferding of South Elmham!) In addition to this there were 239 sheep, 15 cattle, and 5 horses, needing about 300 acres. This total grassland area of 5,300 acres would leave 3,648 acres for arable use and woodland. The total declared 'acreage' in the Domesday

Book is 2,392. Perhaps the Book makes an assumption, which is not declared, on the acreage of grassland needed to support each plough. The addition of all these acres of grassland would bring the total Domesday area much nearer to the present known acreage of South Elmham. (7,692 acres compared with 8,948 acres respectively)

There are five references to the dimensions of land in and near to South Elmham. They are as follows:

> Flixton (53:5*)   1 league by ½ a league
> Homersfield (19:13*) 1 league by ½ a league
> Elmham (19:14*)   1 league by ½ a league
> Bungay (1:111*)   2 leagues by 1 league 8 furlongs
> Westleton (6:85*)   2 leagues 2 furlongs by 2 leagues
> * Are Domesday Book reference numbers.

Such measurements tempt us to calculate areas. Of these places Homersfield seemed to lend itself to detailed assessment of its area because it was mainly a single manor. (Entry 18:4. see table IV) There are various assessments of the length of a league from 'more than a mile' (The Oxford Companion to Local and Family History), to 1½ miles in a Domesday Book footnote, to the more common 3 miles stated in most encyclopaedias. As the other Homersfield holding 19:13 formed only a small part of the parish in 1086 (162 acres) the comment at the end 'It has 1 league in length and ½ in width' must surely apply to the whole parish. The longest dimension in Homersfield is 1.88 miles. (This is the average of 6 measurements on the Ordnance Survey map) Does this mean our local league is 1.88 miles? This would give Homersfield an area of 1.88 by 0.94 miles, or 1.77 square miles. There are 640 acres in a square mile, giving Homersfield therefore 1,131 acres. But we know that Suckling's assessment was only 981 acres, a discrepancy of 150 acres. Perhaps this error of just over 15% is near enough. If the league was 1½ miles the area of Homersfield would come out at 720 acres, a far greater discrepancy of 261 acres. A further problem arises with the acre, which was not standardised until the 13th century; the 'broad acres' of Yorkshire were equal to two statute acres. Thus attempts like this to unravel the details of Domesday frequently fail, reminding us that the information collected by the commissioners, often against the wishes of the local people, and with ill defined methods of measurement, was primarily to assess the yield of rents and the services due to local land holders, and the taxation due to the king.

Accuracy in land measurement would have been of marginal interest; it was the land's value and ownership that was important. The lack of detail did not prevent assessment of the nameless holdings of named men and women for value, service, or taxes.

The Domesday record does reveal that there is something special about Homersfield. At less than one sixth of the true area of Elmham it had nearly three times its value in the Domesday record. (£14-6s-8d compared with £5-1s respectively, in 1066. Table IV). Darby has found that value can be linked to the number of ploughs, but this does not seem to apply here, Homersfield had 20 and Elmham 32, though the number per square mile, using modern measurement, was 13 for Homersfield and only 3.3 for Elmham. Darby has studied the density of Saxon ploughs in Suffolk and found the greatest was in the heavy clay lands of Claydon (between Ipswich and Needham Market) at 4.4 per square mile and the lowest in Breckland at 0.8. This makes Homersfield very much out of the ordinary range, and suggests that perhaps its boundaries have changed. Looking back at the Domesday acreage and the modern acreage, only one of the three parishes is anywhere near the modern assessment and that is Homersfield, and we know that it also had woodland for 600 pigs. As the land in the other two parishes is so much underestimated in Domesday, (see the table on page 110) perhaps Homersfield was also very much underestimated.

If that parish had been much larger it would probably have included part of what is now St. Cross, possibly with the boundary running along the Beck. This makes it possible that the present site of St. Cross church was in Homersfield and was the second church in that parish, part of a small manor worked by a freeman under the patronage of bishop Aelmer. (Part of holding number 9:13 See Table IV) The endowment of this second church was quite generous at 30 acres; in 1846 St. Cross church's glebe was not very different at 25 acres 1 rood and 7 perches.[4] This would have meant that the Minster stood alone as the only church building in what was left of St. Cross. If the northeast part of the boundary had also been a little further south, it would have brought the parish of St. Margaret into contact with all but one of the other eight parishes in the ferding. This would then have been reminiscent of the arrangement of thirteen parishes around North Walsham in Norfolk. This striking arrangement of parochial boundaries Williamson attributes to the breakaway of parishes at the edge of an ancient minsterland.[5] The problem in South Elmham is that 'the minster' is not in St. Margaret but in the peripheral parish of St. Cross, though even here there is some confusion. Gillingwater in describing his visit to The Old Minster in 1804 writes that it lies in St. Margaret, and Suckling also refers to the minster as generally being considered to lie in St. Margaret. This tradition raises the possibility that St. Margaret's parish's strange extension into St. Cross, to include the ancient site of 'Eldhallestede' and part of the moated site of South Elmham Hall, might not in fact be an extension, but a relic of a much larger parish that included The Old Minster. The parishes of Homersfield and St. Margaret would then have each been partly in place of St. Cross, and St. Cross would not have existed. (See Map I) This would infer that the establishment of the parish of St. Cross (or St. George) was late, and would be in keeping with the late recognition of St. George as the patron saint of England in the early 15th century. Anyway, a dedication to St. George would seem unlikely before the crusades. If in fact the minster had been in this larger St. Margaret's parish, it would be another pointer to its use as an old minster in the later Saxon sense, rather than as a monastery, and would have served its 'parochia' of the nine communities indicated by Domesday Book's nine local churches. Perhaps, as Blair suggests, there was no clear distinction between monasteries and minsters, even those monks who were dedicated to devotion and learning had pastoral duties.[6]

Homersfield was mainly a single manor of high value in the lordship of Aelmer, Bishop of Elmham. (£12-6-8d compared with £5-1-0d for Elmham and £3-16-6d for Flixton. See Table XI) It had a mill, and probably had the only easy crossing point over the Waveney for miles up and down the river. The feld element in Homersfield suggests a clearing in a landscape of predominant woodland, and wood pasture for 600 pigs was far in excess of any of the other local assessments except for Mendham. Mendham was also a high valued single manor owned by the bishop, with 598 pigs, and 2 $1/4$ churches, worth £10-11-6d. (See tables VI, VII, & VIII.) There is yet another high value parish in the adjacent Bishop's Hundred at Hoxne. This important manor was just over 1000 acres, had woodland for 250 pigs, two mills, and a Saturday market. It was valued at £28 in 1066. Hoxne was important because it had been the site of Theodred's bishopric of Suffolk, and was still the seat of the bishopric in 1066. The Domesday entry includes this sentence; 'In this manor is a church, the Episcopal see of Suffolk 'Tempore Regis Edwardi' or in King Edward's time. (For further discussion on this see pages 37-38, 46, and 93).

Some idea of the structure of the population in South Elmham can be gained from the Domesday record. It lists those in each rank of the eleventh century society. Nearly all of them are men, only rarely are women mentioned. The following table uses the actual figures quoted in the record for 1066 and Suckling's statements of areas for calculating the population per square mile:

	Flixton	Homersfield	Elmham	Totals
Freemen	17	24	60	101
Villagers	16	16	16	48
Smallholders	21	14	28	63
Slaves	2	4	5	11
Totals	56	58	109	223
Pop. Per Sq. Mile	28.1	40	11.9	15.9

For the whole of South Elmham the density of population is 15.9 per square mile and roughly the same as Darby calculated for the hundred of Wangford at 16.6. The table above once again marks Homersfield as being very different from the other places with a density more than twice the average. Both Flixton and Homersfield are much more populous than Elmham. The table below compares the relative numbers of the various ranks in the societies of South Elmham and the whole of rural Suffolk that Darby has studied.[7]

	Rural Suffolk	% of total	South Elmham	% of total
Freemen	8589	44.9	101	45
Villagers	3130	16.3	48	21.5
Smallholders	6460	33.8	63	28.3
Slaves	34	4.7	11	4.9

Except therefore for a slight difference in the proportions of the villagers and the smallholders, South Elmham differs little from the rest of rural Suffolk. For a general comparison of the Domesday figures for South Elmham, Flixton, Homersfield, Mendham, and Ilketshall, see Table XI.

The population figures used in these calculations are those quoted in The Domesday Book. It has been suggested that increasing this recorded number by a factor of 3.5 gives a better idea of the total population. Doing that for the whole of South Elmham gives a figure of 780 (3.5 x 223) for 1066 AD.

Some details of the lives of landholders in and near to South Elmham.

There are some important pre-Conquest personal names both as holders of land, and giving their names to the land, in and near to South Elmham. Bishops Felix and Hunberht who in all probability are remembered in the

Map VI

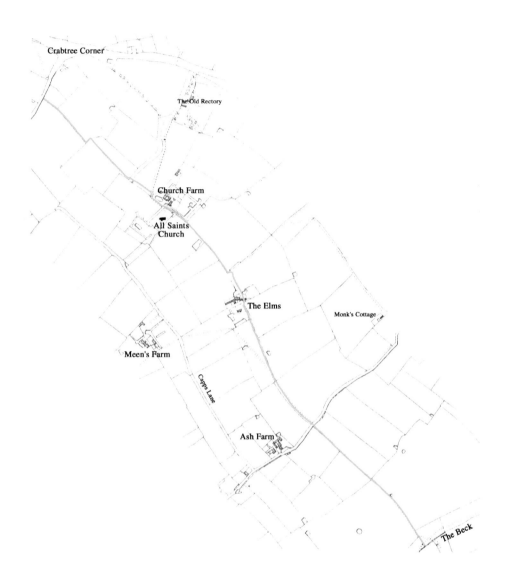

Footpath from the St. Nicholas road near to Crabtree Corner, to the Beck near the Rumburgh border. It passes between All Saints Churchyard and the moated manor house site of Church Farm, following the waving line of the ancient field boundaries.

Based on the 1905 6 inch Ordnance Survey sheets 17 at Lowestoft Record Office

Plate XXVI

The 1856 reconstructed Flixton church tower, and a
close view showing the reuse of the old stone balusters
from the Saxon tower.

Plate XXVII

The Saxon tower of Sompting church in East Sussex

Plate XXIX

All Saints Church May 2003.

Plate XXX

All Saints church, the interior of the west end showing
some of the features that may be Saxon.

Plate XXXI

Reused stonework around the chancel door at St. Michael's Church South Elmham

Plate XXXII

St. Michael's church south door.
Is this a Norman insert in a Saxon wall?

Plate XXXIII

Archbishop Stigand at the coronation of King Harold,
as shown on the Bayeux Tapestry.

names of Flixton and Homersfield respectively, are discussed elsewhere in detail. (See pages 32, and 103.)

Ulfcytel.

Ilketshall is mentioned for the first time in the Domesday Book, where it is written in two forms: Ilcheteshala and Ilcheteleshala. It was probably Suckling who first wrote of the likelihood of the name having its origin in the 11th century heroic figure of **Ulfcytel**.[8] Norman Scarfe has suggested that though his 'hall' might have been at 'The Mount', a man made mound in Ilketshall St. John, it was more likely to have been in the naturally defensive position of Bungay.[9] Freeman makes him an Earldorman by implication because he is known to have summoned the local Witan, (local assembly).[10] In 1004 Swein Forkbeard, or Swegen, king of Denmark *'came with his fleet to Norwich and raided and burned down the town.'* Ulfcytel with his councillors bought peace to reduce further damage, because they had been taken by surprise, and his army was not ready. In spite of this Swein within three weeks moved on Thetford, and raided and burned down that town. In the meantime Ulfcytel, knowing of this evil act, sent men to destroy Swein's ships, and confronted Swein's men in bloody battle. There was great slaughter on both sides, and the *'chief men of the East Anglian people'* were killed except for their leader Ulfcytel. Swein's ships were never destroyed because Ulcytel's men failed him, and Swein held the day, but admitted that if Ulfcytel's army had been up to strength he would never have returned to his ships. They had never met with harder *hand play* in England than Ulfcytel had given them.[11] A Danish saga gave him the name Snilling meaning bold or quick, and described East Anglia as Ulfkelsland.[10] Freeman goes on to say that *'Ulfcytel's name proclaims his Danish origin but it was in him that England now found her stoutest champion in her hour of need'*.[12] Swein Forkbeard was to become king of England and was the father of the future great King Cnut. Ulfcytel was destined to come into a fatal conflict with Cnut at the battle of Ashingdon in Essex in 1016. In this year Cnut's raiding army travelled into Mercia and savagely raided there, provoking King Edmund Ironside into *'assembling the entire English Nation for the fifth time'* and follow Cnut's army into Essex, and here they resolutely joined battle. But among the English forces was the unreliable Earldoman Eadric Streona whose men ran from the battlefield as they had done before *'betraying his royal lord and the whole Nation of the English race.'* Cnut won the day and *the Nation of the English*. All the 'chief men' of the English Nation died including Ulfcytel, but not Edmund Ironside himself who later met Cnut on an island in the River Severn where they became 'pledge brothers' dividing England between them. This lasted only a month or so, for on St. Andrew's day (30th November) Edmund died and Cnut ruled alone.[13] Here, in the passing of Ulfcytel, is the fragmentary story of this turncoat Dane who became our greatest local pre Conquest warrior and hero.

Gyrth.

It seems a reasonable assumption that the lands in Ilketshall under the control of Hugh Bigod in 1086 had before 1066 belonged to Gyrth, Earl of The East Angles, and brother of King Harold Godwinson. Having shared in the king's victory at Stamford Bridge over Harold Hardrada, Gyrth fought most boldly beside his two brothers at Hastings. As William himself approached the three brothers, it was Gyrth who pressed forward throwing the spear that unhorsed William. The Duke was well able to fight on foot, in fact it gave him opportunity to move forward and confront the man who had unhorsed him. With a mighty head blow from the duke's mace Gyrth's bold and brave defence of his royal brother ended. Leofwine his other brother died at his side at the hand of another Norman, leaving Harold, still the dominant force on the field, to fight on without them.[14]

Stigand.

Stigand, Bishop of Elmham, 1042-1047 was a very different man indeed, and a large landowner in South Elmham. James Campbell thinks he might have been a local boy, possibly from Norwich, who did well, (he gives nothing to support this idea), but goes on to claim, with good reason, that he was perhaps the most successful cleric in the long history of the English church.[15] The first records of him are in 1020 when Cnut built a stone minster in remembrance of the men killed at the battle of Ashingdon in Essex and *'gave it to his own priest whose name was Stigand'*.[16] He became exceedingly wealthy, owning much land in East Anglia. In 1038 he had been appointed bishop of Selsey (West Sussex), but before consecration he was deposed by another who was prepared to offer more money for the post, but then finally reinstated.[17] In 1042 he was made bishop of Elmham, and at that time would have had his seat at North Elmham. A year later he was deprived of this post because of his support for Queen Emma. Emma was the daughter of Duke Richard I of Normandy and was first married to Aethelred the Unready of England by whom she had two sons Alfred and Edward, and secondly to Cnut. Emma was implicated in the death of Alfred, and in having made poison with the intention of dispatching Edward who later became King Edward the Confessor. As a result of this Stigand was deprived of his bishopric and Emma put to trial by ordeal. In the legend of this trial she was made to walk over four burning ploughshares. This she did successfully. All was forgiven, and Stigand's bishopric of Elmham was restored to him. Freeman reviews the accounts of these events, which are neither as reliable nor as simple as suggested here.[18]

In 1047 Stigand was made bishop of Winchester. In 1052 Earl Godwine and his family's military challenge to the authority of King Edward was defused on the banks of the Thames in London, at least in part by the mediation of Stigand. The Normans, whom Edward had appointed to many powerful positions including the archbishopric of Canterbury, were banished. Stigand filled this vacancy at Canterbury without leaving his bishopric of Winchester, thus adding to his sin of simony (the selling of pardons) the sin of holding bishoprics in 'plurality'. Stigand seemed always to be at the centre of controversy, a man of great wealth and power, infinite guile, and no doubt great charm. He had a position of some influence at the Abbey of Ely, and to this foundation he is said to have given a life-sized silver crucifix and a life-sized silver statue of Christ. In 1058 the usurper Pope Benedict X sent Stigand the pallium, or cloak of his office of archbishop, possibly by the hand of Harold Godwinson himself who happened to be on a pilgrimage to Rome.[19] This was of doubtful advantage to Stigand, for, when on the 5th of January 1066 Harold Godwinson was crowned king of England, Florence of Worcester wrote that it was not Stigand but Archbishop Aldred of York who placed the crown on his head.[20] Neither had Harold asked him to consecrate his new abbey at Waltham. On the other hand, William of Poitiers asserted that Harold had been crowned by the unholy Stigand and was therefore unfit to rule.[21] The Bayeux Tapestry shows, very clearly, Stigand, with his tonsured curly blond hair holding the maniple, standing by Harold's left hand at his coronation. (See Plate XXXIII) This feature of the work both Freeman and Stenton attribute to Norman propaganda. David Wilson however considers this an unlikely thesis.[22] Freeman has the best and most closely argued reasoning, and concludes that it was Aldred that crowned Harold.[23]

Aldred, Archbishop of York, also crowned William on Christmas day after the Battle of Hastings. At the ceremony Aldred and Stigand stood either side of William as he walked to his throne. In 1067 Stigand went with King William to Normandy, and on his return appointed the first Norman Bishop to the See of Dorchester (on Thames). (This was Remigius who had been the almoner at Fecamp Abbey, where the future bishop of Norwich, Herbert de Losinga was prior.) William continued to let the well-organised English state run itself, but men like Stigand must have been aware that their days of power were numbered. The Papal influence was much stronger under William and eventually, by 1070, legates from Rome arrived and courts were held at Winchester where Stigand appeared and perhaps made no defence. No record of the trial survives. It seems likely that he lived his final years comfortably. The Domesday Book records him owning the large manor of East Meon (West of Petersfield in Hampshire) worth £40 a year until his death in 1072.[24] William of Malmsbury gives us a more colourful end to the story. He claimed that he was imprisoned in Winchester and lived there as an ascetic, and when encouraged to eat more by a friend he said that he had not a penny to supply his wants. He kept a key hanging around his neck, and when he died this was found to unlock a writing case, inside this were the details of the location of a great hoard of buried treasure.[25]

Stigand's brother was called **Aethelmaer** or **Aelmer**, he was married and this marriage had brought him land at Blofield in Norfolk[26] More land came to him from his brother, and no doubt his brother's influence helped him to take over the bishopric of Elmham, which became vacant when Stigand went to Winchester in 1047. Aelmer held land in both North and South Elmham, (See Table XII for his North Elmham holdings) and continued to acquire land, some by purchase, some by forfeiture, in one case because the previous owner had sinned by remarrying within a year of her husband's death. In another case he acquired 4½ acres of land after King Edward's Captain of ships, a man called Eadric, had been outlawed by William for supporting Harold at Hastings.[27] Stigand took land from a man called Ailwy and gave it to Ailmer, but witnesses said they did not know how this had come about.[28] Was this all sheer unfeeling greed for land, or was it part of a planned acquisition of land to boost the wealth of the Diocese? Many of the acquisitions occurred after the Conquest, and Aelmer may have foreseen, in those very troubled times of his later years, that the best he could do was to accumulate land for the benefit of the diocese. The diocese of Elmham was one of the largest in England, and yet by comparison with the two great abbeys of Ely, and Bury St. Edmund's, it had been poor. It had no buildings large enough to assemble its clergy, and as Campbell points out the territory was too large for the bishop to keep in touch with all his parishes.[29] Perhaps, therefore, the two brothers, Stigand and Aelmer, by their acquisitive behaviour made it easier for the third

Norman bishop, Herbert de Losinga, to build the great cathedral at Norwich. We know, however, that Herbert had to raise a great deal more money from various sources including a special tax for the building, and was rather surprisingly also given revenue from taxes originally set up to pay for the building of Bury St. Edmund's Abbey. Aelmer was finally deposed in 1070 and the lands he had acquired for himself since 1066 were added to the property of the see of Elmham. This gave the see a more even spread of possessions throughout Norfolk than hitherto, and left Suffolk with its ancient possessions mainly along the Waveney valley at Elmham and in the Bishop's Hundred which included Hoxne.

Six freemen are named as landholders in South Elmham. Their names are **Godric, Offa, Alwyn, Askell, Bondi, Alwy,** and **Brictnoth**. There was one thane with the obviously Scandinavian name of **Ingvar**. Where are these names now? Alwyn occurs once in the local telephone directory as a surname, and Bondi twice, but none of the others. We know nothing of these men except that some of them may have held land elsewhere.

The Norman takeover of the lands of South Elmham and its surrounding areas is well recorded in the Domesday Book. The process must have been a painful one for the English. The new landowners would have been quick to demonstrate their authority, no doubt by arrogance, by the building of fortifications, the rebuilding of the local churches, and the increased taxation shown in the Domesday records. Whereas there had been two languages, English, and in the church Latin, now there were three. Norman French would have prevented direct communication between the Conquerors and the English. The heroic figures of King Harold and his brother Gyrth, Earl of the East Angles, who died at Hastings, lost their estates to the new king and his sheriff Hugh Bigod. Edric of Laxfield's vast estates were taken by William Malet, who, by 1072, had built his castle in them at Eye. In south Elmham itself the big change was from ownership by Aelmer and Stigand, to ownership by William the new Norman bishop who had set up his see at Thetford. Count Alan (of Brittany) was the son-in-law of King William and the new owner of a small holding (3:105) in Elmham, which belonged to the church in Rumburgh. Another small holding (6:298) was taken by Robert Malet who on his father (William's) death became lord of Eye. William Malet is said to have had an English mother, and had been one of William the Conqueror's leaders at Hastings. After this terrible event it is said that an area in the battlefield was cleared of dead bodies so that duke William could have a midnight meal. Among these bodies was that of King Harold, but it had been so mutilated by the vengeance of the Normans that it was unrecognisable to all save Eadgyth of the Swan Neck, his mistress. She bravely searched through the dead and eventually found Harold's body. The body was wrapped in a purple cloth, but William forbade a Christian burial. It was William Malet who eventually took the body and buried it beneath a pile of stones. The body was later 'translated' to Harold's Abbey at Waltham. William Malet later survived a defeat by the Danes in York, but was killed fighting Hereward at Ely in 1072.[30]

This chapter began by exposing some of the difficulties of trying to understand The Domesday Book, but later, I hope, showed how rewarding certain approaches to the interpretation of its contents can be. The big discrepancy between the stated acreage and the actual land area, the unusual status of Homersfield suggesting that parish boundaries may not have been static, the structure of the local population, and some of the famous local land owners and their exploits, are reviewed.

[1] Domesday Book. Suffolk. Phillimore & Co. Ltd. 1984.

[2] H.C.Darby. *The Domesday Geography of Eastern England*. Cambridge Univ. Press. (1971) pp. 157

[3] Oliver Rackham. The History of the Countryside. Phoenix Giant Paperback. (1986) p. 335

[4] Alfred Suckling. *History of the County of Suffolk*. Vol. 1 (1846) p.211

[5] Tom Williamson. *The Origins of Norfolk*. Manchester University Press. (1993) p. 152 & figure 6.2

[6] John Blair. 'Minster Churches in the Landscape', Anglo-Saxon Settlements. Ed. Della Hooke. Basil Blackwell Ltd. (1988) pp.35-40

[7] Darby H.C. Domesday Geography of Eastern England. 3rd Edition. (1971) p.169

[8] Alfred Suckling. *History of the County of Suffolk*. Vol. 1. (1846) p. 111

[9] Norman Scarfe. *The Suffolk Landscape*. Alastair Press. (1987) p.109

[10] E.A. Freeman. *The History of The Norman Conquest of England*. Second Edition. Vol. I. (1870) p. 639

[11] The Anglo-Saxon Chronicles. Peterborough Manuscript (E) for 1004 AD

[12] E.A. Freeman *The History of The Norman Conquest of England*. Second Edition Vol I (1870) p. 319

[13] The Anglo-Saxon Chronicles. Canterbury Manuscript (F) for 1016.

[14] E.A. Freeman. *The History of The Norman Conquest of England*. First Edition Vol. III (1869) pp. 484-486

[15] James Campbell. 'The East Anglian Sees Before the Conquest' *Norwich Cathedral. Church, City, and Diocese* 1096-1996. (1996) p. 18

[16] Florence of Worcester. Chronicon ex Chronicis as a footnote in Worcester Manuscript D for 1020 in The Anglo-Saxon Chronicles.

[17] Florence of Worcester quoted by Freeman in *The History of The Norman Conquest*. Second Revised Edition. Vol. I. (1870) p. 501

[18] E.A.Freeman *The History of the Norman Conquest of England*. Second Edition Revised. Vol. II. (1870) Note H. pp.569-71

[19] Ibid. Vol. II pp. 431-3

[20] The Anglo-Saxon Chronicles. Abingdon Manuscript (C) 1066. & Worcester Manuscript (D) 1065 Footnote 2

[21] Quoted by Sir Frank Stenton in *Anglo-Saxon England*. The Oxford History of England. 3rd Ed. Clarenden Press. (1971) p. 466

[22] David Wilson. *The Bayeux Tapestry*. Thames and Hudson. 1985.

[23] E.A. Freeman *The History of The Norman Conquest of England*. First Edition. Vol. III. (1869) Note D pp. 612-622

[24] Sir Frank Stenton. *Anglo-Saxon England*. The Oxford History of England. 3rd. Ed. Clareden Press. (1971) pp. 660-661 & footnote 1 on p.661

[25] William of Malmsbury. *Gesta Pontificum*. 37. 1125 AD.

[26] Domesday Book. Norfolk. Folio 195a 10:28

[27] Ibid. Folio 200 10:77

[28] Ibid. Folio 195a 10:30

[29] James Campbell. 'The East Anglian Sees Before the Conquest' *Norwich Cathedral Church City and Diocese 1096-1996*. (1996) p.19

[30] E.A.Freeman. *History of the Norman Conquest of England*. First Edition. Vol. IV. (1871) pp. 269, & 473 footnote 2

An Enigma of Ancient Suffolk

Epilogue

This study of the early history of South Elmham has been built on a minimum of good firm evidence, and a liberal weave of speculation. The few early written sources were often produced hundreds of years after the events they describe, or they were biased to champion some long forgotten cause. The archaeological evidence is scanty. Hardly anything is certain, and so it seems reasonable to suspect anyone who claims to know the answers.

Speculation, even wild speculation, nevertheless has virtue. This lies in the production of ideas, both good and bad, from which informed choices can be made to illuminate our vision of the past. In this text I have tried to include many of the ideas of expert historians, and some of the ideas that I think are my own. After reading a great amount on the subject it becomes difficult to disentangle my own thoughts from those of others who might have stimulated them. If I have failed to attribute any ideas to their true originator I apologise sincerely, but the importance is in the collection and accurate record of this information. This I hope will have been found in this little book, and that it will give the reader the opportunity to heartily disagree or agree, and perhaps make further contributions to our understanding of this historically neglected patch of Suffolk.

Appendix A

A field trip to The Old Minster on April 4th 2002

This trip was made to witness sunrise from The Old Minster site, and measure its bearing and timing. The information was then used to check the validity of the software prediction (using 'Redshift 2' published by Maris Multimedia Ltd. 1993-5).

Sunrise is normally considered to occur when the upper limb of the sun first shows above the horizon. On this occasion the sun was not visible until its whole disc was suddenly revealed sitting on the slightly misty horizon at 6.35 am on a corrected bearing of 82° 25'.

The Redshift 2 software predicted that the whole sun would be above the horizon as I saw it at 6.35 on a bearing of 82° 07', an error of only 18' (less than half a degree) This confirmed the accuracy of the method, but of course did not test the software's ability to correct for changes caused by new calendars, precession, or nutation over the last 1000 years. These things I have taken on trust.

Appendix and Tables

Appendix B

Field trip to The Old Minster on February 16th 2002

This visit was made by my son Dr William Harrold and myself. We measured the orientation and coordinates of the ruin, and the elevation of the horizon in the line of its orientation.

The orientation was derived from the magnetic bearings taken looking east along the outside of the south wall of the ruin, and then west. These two bearings were 62.5° and 242.5° respectively.

Calculating true north from magnetic north was troublesome. The Ordnance Survey Explorer map 231 indicates that "at the centre of this sheet true north is 2° 48' west of grid north. Magnetic north is 6' west of grid north for 1999 decreasing by about 0.5° in 4 years." However the Ordnance Survey Landranger map 156 states that magnetic north is 6° west of grid north, and this is confirmed on the internet at http://www.geo-orbit.org/sizepgs/magmapsp.htm#anchor601698 which indicates about 6° for 1995. The 6' on the Explorer map is therefore a misprint.

Using the OS Landranger map 156 the calculations are as follows:

1. Magnetic north varies with place and time. The direction for the centre of the sheet (where The Old Minster is) was about 6°(107 mils) west of grid north in 1998, decreasing by about 0.5° (9 mils) in every 4 years. There are 6,400 mils in a full circle so one degree is 17.77 mils. From say June 1998 to February 2002 is 3.67 years, this would mean that magnetic north had moved to the east by 3.67/4 x 9 mils = 8.25 mils. This gives it the new position of 5.55° west of grid north.

2. Returning now to the OS Explorer map 231, at its centre where The Old Minster is, true north is 2° 48' (2.80°) west of grid north. Therefore magnetic north is 5.55°-2.80° = 2.75° west of true north.

3. The true orientation of The Old Minster is therefore 62.5°-2.75°= 59.75°.

4. The coordinates of The Old Minster are those produced by a hand held geopositioning device (Garmin GPS III). They are for the centre of the ruin:

    52° 23.60' north.
    01° 23.39' east.

5. Elevation of the horizon. This was measured using a 1-metre spirit level with a quoted accuracy of 0.057°, or 1 mm. in 1 metre. Attached to this as a sight line was another straight edge measuring 847mm. Both these were set up within the site of The Old Minster. With the spirit level horizontal and the straight edge aligned to the eastern horizon, and both in line with the orientation of The Old Minster, the end of the straight edge was elevated 12.5 mm. The elevation of the horizon was therefore $(360/2\pi)$ x $(12.5+$ or-$1) \div 847 = +0.854° +$ or- 0.067

6. When this information was fed into the Redshift 2 software using the date of 1000AD, the spring day on which the sun would have risen in that year in line with the orientation of The Old Minster was May 7th. With each change forward of 100 years, this date goes back by one day. Therefore in 1100 it would have been May 6th, and for 900 May 8th.

Appendix and Tables

Table I

Name DB Ref.	Elmham 13:6	Elmham 13:6	Elmham 19:16	Elmham 19:16	Elmham 19:16	Elmham 19:16
Lordship or Patronage	Ralph the Constable	Ralph the Constable	Ingvar a thane	Bishop Aelmer	Bishop Aelmer	A.Bishop Stigand
As manor	Yes			Yes		Yes
Carucates			2			
Acres	40	5	20	60	7	30
Freemen	Godric	2 under Godric	Alwin	Bondi	2 under Bondi	1
Villagers	2		10	2		2
Smallholders	1		11	2		
Slaves	1		4			
Ploughs		1/2			1	1
Ploughs Lord	1		3	1		
Ploughs Men	1/2		6	1		1
Wood pigs	4		30			8
Meadow acres	2		11	2		2
Cobs			1			
Sheep			13			
Cattle			7			
Pigs			30			
Goats			30			
Mills	1/5					
Churches	1 and 1/5		1			
Church acres	8 and 6		40 1/2plough			
Church Value	12d					
Value 1066	7s			>	10s	8s
Value 1086	20s	>	£4	>	13s	10s 8d
Tax						

A Summary of the Domesday Book Record for part of South Elmham for 1066

An Enigma of Ancient Suffolk

Table II

Name	Elmham	Elmham	Elmham	Elmham	Elmham	Elmham
DB Ref	19:16	19:16	19:16	19:14	19:14	19:14
Lordship	Edric of Laxfield	Edric of Laxfield	Bishop Aelmer	Bishop Aelmer	Bishop Aelmer	Bishop Aelmer
As manor	Yes			Yes	Yes	
Carucates			1 1/2			
Acres	30	4		40+6	40	66
Freemen	Alwy	2 under Alwy	25	1 + 3 under him	Alwin	10
Villagers						
Smallholders	2			4	2	
Slaves						
Ploughs	1/2	1/2	8	1 + 1/2	1	1
Ploughs Lord						
Ploughs Men						
Wood pigs	8		16	8		
Meadow acres	1		6	2	2	2
Cobs						
Sheep						
Cattle						
Pigs						
Goats						
Mills						
Churches			3	1		
Church acres			30	6		
Church Value			5s			
Value 1066	>	10s	30s	10s	6s	10s
Value 1086	>	10s	40s	12s	10s 8d	14s
Tax						

A Summary of the Domesday Book Record for part of South Elmham for 1066

Table III

Namef DB Re	Elmham 19:14	Elmham 3:105*	Elmham 6:298	TOTALS
Lordship	Bishop Aelmer	Ralph the Constable	Edric of Laxfield?	
As manor				6
Carucates				3^1/$_2$
Acres	34	40	15	437
Freemen	10			61
Villagers				16
Smallholders		6		28
Slaves				5
Ploughs	3	1		19
Ploughs Lord				5
Ploughs Men				8^1/$_2$
Wood pigs		6		80
Meadow acres				30
Cobs				1
Sheep				13
Cattle				7
Pigs				30
Goats				30
Mills				1/5
Churches				6 1/5
Church acres				90
Church Value				6s
Value 1066	10s			£5 1s
Value 1086	20s		2s 6d	£11 12s 10d
Tax	20d			20d

A Summary of the Domesday Book Record for South Elmham in 1066 including totals

*This land belongs to the church in Rumburgh. Holding 3:14 in Wissett includes a church with 12 monks, and under it one chapel with 2 carucates of free land, all held by Ralph the Constable

Table IV

Name DB Ref	Homersfield 18:4	Homersfield 19:13	Homersfield 19:13	Totals
Lordship	Bishop Aelmer	Bishop Aelmer	Bishop Aelmer	TOTALS
As manor	Yes	Yes		2
Carucates	5			5
Acres		40	80	120
Freemen		1	23	24
Villagers	16			16
Smallholders	12	2		14
Slaves	4			4
Ploughs		2	6	8
Ploughs Lord	2			2
Ploughs Men	10			10
Wood pigs	600			600
Meadow acres	12	2		14
Cobs	3			3
Sheep	200			200
Cattle	6			6
Pigs	26			26
Goats				
Mills	1			1
Churches	1	1		2
Church acres	12	30		42
Church Value				
Value 1066	£12	6s 8d	£2	£14 6 8d
Value 1086	£16	9s 4d	£1 10s	£17 19 4d
Tax		>	20d	20d

A Summary of the Domesday Book Record for Homersfield for 1066

Table V

Name DB Ref.	Flixton 53:5	Flixton 53:5	Flixton 19:15	Flixton 19:15	Flixton 19:17	Flixton 19:17	Flixton 19:17	Flixton 19:17	Totals
Lordship	Bishop Stigand	Bishop Stigand	Bishop Stigand	Bishop Aelmer	Bishop Aelmer	Bishop Aelmer	Bishop Stigand	Bishop Stigand	Totals
As manor		Yes	Yes		Yes		Yes		4
Carucates		2							2
Acres	30		30	107	30	38	30	16	281
Freemen	2	1 Offa	1 Askell	8	1 Brictnoth	3	1	1	18
Villagers		16							16
Smallhold	3$^1/_2$	11	1		4		2		21$^1/_2$
Slaves		2							2
Ploughs	2$^1/_2$		1	2	1	1$^1/_2$	1	$^1/_2$	9$^1/_2$
Ploughs Lord		2							2
Ploughs Men		13$^1/_2$			$^1/_2$				14
Wood pigs	2	20			4	4	4		34
Meadow acres	3$^1/_2$	12	2		2	3	2		24$^1/_2$
Cobs		1							1
Sheep		26							26
Cattle		2							2
Pigs									
Goats									
Mills		$^1/_2$	1/5						7/10
Churches		$^1/_2$		$^1/_2$					1
Church acres		10		12					22
Church value		16d							16d
Value 1066	7s	40s	8s	10s	5s 4d	6s		10s	£4 6s 4d
Value 1086	10s 8d	£3	10s 8d	£1 11s 4d	£1	11s 8d		10s	£7 4s 4d
Tax	20d								20d

A Summary of The Domesday Book Record for Flixton
in the Wangford Hundred for the year 1066

An Enigma of Ancient Suffolk

Table VI

Name DB Ref	Mendham 14:106	Mendham 14:106	Mendham 4:106	Mendham 8:42	Mendham 8:42
Lordship Jurisdiction	St. Edmund Abbey	St. Edmund Abbey	St. Edmund Abbey	Bishop's Manor of Hoxne	Bishop's Manor of Hoxne
As manor	Yes				
Carucates	2	1/2		1	
Acres	19		3		18
Freemen		6	1	3	3
Villagers	2			1	
Smallholders	18			6	
Slaves	1				
Ploughs		3			1/2
Ploughs Lord	2				
Ploughs Men	6				
Wood pigs	360	3		60	
Meadow acres	18	2		5	
Cobs	1				
Sheep	40				
Cattle	10				
Pigs	41				
Goats	36				
Mills	1				
Churches		1			
Church acres		20			
Church Value					
Value 1066		£4 10s	6d		£2 16s
Value 1086		£12 4s			
Tax		15d			

A Summary of the Domesday Book Record for
Mendham in the Bishop's Hundred for the year 1066

Appendix and Tables

Table VII

Name DB Ref	Mendham 6:313	Mendham 6:313	Mendham 6:72	Mendham 19:2
Lordship Jurisdiction	In Hoxne	In Hoxne	Bishop Aelmer	Ulf a thane
As manor				
Carucates	1			1
Acres	3	12	10	11
Freemen	1+1 under him	1	1	2
Villagers				1
Smallholders	5			10
Slaves				
Ploughs				
Ploughs Lord	1			1
Ploughs Men	2			$3^{1}/_{2}$
Wood pigs	100			60
Meadow acres	5		$^{1}/_{2}$	6
Cobs				
Sheep				
Cattle				
Pigs				
Goats				
Mills				1
Churches	1+ 1/8			1/8
Church acres	8 + 5			40 + $^{1}/_{2}$ a plough
Church Value				
Value 1066	>	£1 5s		£1 10s
Value 1086	>	£1 10s	2s	£3
Tax				

A Summary of the Domesday Book Record for
Mendham, in the Bishop's Hundred for the year 1066

Table VIII

Name DB Ref	Mendham 10:32 (Norfolk)	Mendham 13:1	TOTALS
Lordship	Bishop Aelmer	Bishop Aelmer	
As manor			1
Carucates			5$\frac{1}{2}$
Acres		4	80
Freemen			19
Villagers			4
Smallholders	3	1	43
Slaves			1
Ploughs	1		4$\frac{1}{2}$
Ploughs Lord			4
Ploughs Men			11$\frac{1}{2}$
Wood pigs	15		598
Meadow acres	3		39$\frac{1}{2}$
Cobs			1
Sheep			40
Cattle			10
Pigs			41
Goats			36
Mills			2
Churches	1 Priest Algar		2$\frac{1}{4}$ + 1 Priest
Church acres	43		116
Church Value			
Value 1066	10s		£10 11s 6d
Value 1086	10s	1s	£17 7s
Tax			15d

A Summary of the Domesday Book Record for
Mendham, in the Bishop's Hundred for the year 1066

Table IX

Name DB Ref	Ilketshall 4:20	Ilketshall 4:22	Ilketshall* 4: 23	Ilketshall 4:24	Ilketshall 4:26
Lordship Patronage	Earl Gyrth Gyrth	Earl Gyrth Wulfsi	Earl Gyrth Wulfsi	Earl Gyrth	Burghard
As manor	Yes	Yes		Yes	
Carucates	2			2	
Acres		60	80		20
Freemen	1 Wulfsi	1 Alwy	7	1 Burghard	1 Freewoman
Villagers	5			5	
Smallholders	13	10	1	7	5
Slaves	6	1		5	
Ploughs			3		
Ploughs Lord	3	1		3	1
Ploughs Men	2	1		3	1
Wood pigs	10	10		30	10
Meadow acres	4	2	2	4	$1^1/_2$
Cobs				2	
Sheep	30			60	
Cattle				2	
Pigs	5				
Goats	16				
Mills	$^1/_2$				
Churches					1
Church acres					20
Church Value					2s
Value 1066	£2	10s	10s	£1 10s	5s
Value 1086	£2	10s	10s	£2	5s
Tax					

A Summary of the Domesday Book Record for
Ilketshall in the hundred of Wangford for the year 1066

*Also in Mettingham and Shipmeadow

Table X

Name DB Ref	lketshall 4:28	Ilketshall* 4:32	Ilketshall* 4:32	Ilketshall 13:7	TOTALS
Lordship Patronage	Earl Gyrth Burghard	Earl Gyrth	Earl Gyrth	GodrictheSteward Edwin	
As manor					3
Carucates					4
Acres	30	12	10	30	242
Freemen	3	1	1	1 Anund	16 and 1 freewoman
Villagers					10
Smallholders				5	41
Slaves					12
Ploughs	1				4
Ploughs Lord				1	9
Ploughs Men				1/2	71/2
Wood pigs					60
Meadow acres				1	141/2
Cobs					2
Sheep					90
Cattle					2
Pigs					5
Goats					16
Mills					1/2
Churches					1
Church acres					20
Church Value					2s
Value 1066	5s			8s 4d	£5 8s 4d
Value 1086	5s			10s	£6
Tax					

A Summary of the Domesday Book Record for Ilketshall
in the Wangford Hundred for the year 1066

*Here the ownership was complex

Table XI

Name	Elmham S	FlixtonW	Homersfield	Mendham	Ilketshall
Manors	6	4	2	1	3
Carucates	3½	2	5	5½	4
Acres	437	281	120	80	242
Freemen	61	18	24	19	16 and 1 woman
Villagers	16	16	16	4	10
Smallholders	28	21½	14	43	41
Slaves	5	2	4	1	12
Ploughs	19	9	8	4½	4
Ploughs Lord	5	3	2	4	9
Ploughs Men	8½	14	10	11½	7½
Wood pigs	80	34	600	598	60
Meadow acres	30	24½	14	39½	14½
Cobs	1	1	3	1	2
Sheep	13	26	200	40	90
Cattle	7	2	6	10	2
Pigs	30		26	41	5
Goats	30			36	16
Mills	1/5	7/10	1	2	½
Churches	6 1/5	1	2	2¼ +1priest	1
Church acres	90	22	42	116	20
Church Value	6s	16d			2s
Value 1066	£5 1s	£4 6s 4d	£14 6s 8d	£10 11s 6d	£5 8s 4d
Value 1086	£11 10s 4d	£7 4s 4d	£17 19s 4d	£17 7s	£6
Tax	20d	20d	20d	15d	

A Summary of the Domesday Book Record for
five local parishes for 1066.

Table XII

Name DB Ref	N. Elmham 10:5 Norfolk	N. Elmham 10:5 Norfolk	N. Elmham 10:5 Norfolk	N. Elmham 10:5 Norfolk	TOTALS
Lordship Jurisdiction	BishopAelmer	BishopAelmer BishopStigand	BishopAelmer BishopStigand	BishopAelmer BishopStigand	
Outlier		(Mileham)	Beetley	Beetley	
As manor	Yes				1
Carucates	8	1	1		10
Acres				26	26
Freemen		24		1	25
Villagers	41		7		48
Smallholders	63				63
Slaves	6				6
Ploughs		4		1	5
Ploughs Lord	4		1 could be 2		5
Ploughs Men	16		2		18
Wood pigs	1000	30		5	1035
Meadow acres	24	4	10	1½	39½
Cobs	3				3
Sheep	300				300
Cattle					
Pigs	32				32
Goats	35				35
Mills	4	1			5
Churches	1				1
Church acres	60 + 1 plough				60
ChurchValue	5s 4d				5s 4d
Value 1066	>	>	>	£10	£10
Value 1086	>	>	>	£32	£32
Tax				20d	20d

A Summary of the Domesday Book Record for
North Elmham, in the Launditch Hundred of Norfolk for the year 1066

Index

The figures in *italics* refer to the page numbers of illustrations

Index